PRAISE FOR
STAY HERE WITH ME

"Olmstead offers us one brief, acutely remembered summer between his childhood and young adulthood. Understanding he will never return to work his family's old New Hampshire farm, the leaving is hard. He moves between a deep sense of loss and the guilty promise of a new life. His best friends will stay behind, and his first experience with falling in love, both ecstatic and ravaging, will come to a faltering end. I won't forget his grandfather, a shrewd, demanding and often harsh man, or the boy's fierce and resistant love for him."

—MEREDITH HALL, author of *Beneficence*

"Olmstead grew up in the Sixties and Seventies in rural southern New Hampshire on a farm, a place of unchange, where extraordinary people lived their ordinary lives. By turns heartbreaking and heartwarming, this evocation of a life on the verge of change is exhilarating, and you'll wish you were the eighteen-year-old Robert, crazy in love with Afton and charging ahead into his bright future."

—JOHN DUFRESNE, author of *No Regrets, Coyote*

"Of the many things I love about *Stay Here with Me*, maybe what attracts me above all are the rhythms of the sentences. This is storytelling at its most natural. It's like sitting across the kitchen table from Olmstead deep into a New Hampshire summer night, the six-pack long since finished, and yet you still don't want to get up, you want to keep listening and listening."

—PETER ORNER, author *Still No Word from You*

STAY HERE WITH ME

STAY HERE WITH ME

A MEMOIR

Robert Olmstead

INTRODUCTION BY
BROCK CLARKE

BOSTON
GODINE NONPAREIL

Published in 2024 by
GODINE
Boston, Massachusetts

Cover Photo: *Annemarie.* Copyright © Cig Harvey

First published in 1996 by Metropolitan Books.

LIBRARY OF CONGRESS CATALOGING-IN-PUBLICATION DATA
Names: Olmstead, Robert, author. | Clarke, Brock, author.
Title: Stay here with me : a memoir / Robert Olmstead ; introduction by
    Brock Clarke.
Description: Boston : Godine Nonpareil, 2024. | First published in 1996 by
    Metropolitan Books.
Identifiers: LCCN 2023029119 (print) | LCCN 2023029120 (ebook) | ISBN
    9781567927795 (paperback) | ISBN 9781567927801 (ebook)
Subjects: LCSH: Olmstead, Robert—Childhood and youth. | Authors,
    American—20th century—Biography.
Classification: LCC PS3565.L67 Z474 2024 (print) | LCC PS3565.L67 (ebook)
    | DDC 813/.54 [B]—dc23/eng/20231107
LC record available at https://lccn.loc.gov/2023029119
LC ebook record available at https://lccn.loc.gov/2023029120

First Printing, 2024
Printed in the United States of America

To Jim and Jill and Sam

THE SUICIDES

The tractors at night,
the dimly lighted
kindly lobsters
with glass sides,
with men inside,
and at home wives,
and depression's black dogs
walking out of
the January hedges'
hacked-off sides.

—Jean Valentine

HOME

Breath entering, leaving the leaf,
the lion tense on the branch luxuriant,

the ten-foot drop to
earth, the sail out away, the God-taste—

that's what lights it up,
Nature, and Art: your skin feather to feather
scale to scale with my skin

and the airy sleep, like wine . . .
Two soft old children's books
with red and blue and green crayons still warm on us.

—Jean Valentine

CONTENTS

Introduction

I FIRST MET Robert Olmstead in January 1987. He was the teacher of my introductory fiction workshop at Dickinson College in Carlisle, Pennsylvania. Back then you were allowed to smoke cigarettes in class, and if you were a person like me, you not only smoked cigarettes in class, you chainsmoked cigarettes in class. I should explain what it meant to be a "person like me": a person like me was a person who tried too hard. And I was the worst kind of person who tried too hard: I was the kind of person who didn't know what person I was trying too hard to be, and so I tried too hard to be a lot of them. And one of the people I tried too hard to be was Robert Olmstead.

At that point, Olmstead had written two books—the short story collection *River Dogs* and the novel *Soft Water*—and soon after he would publish his novel *A Trail of Heart's Blood Wherever We Go.* These three books were, and, as far as

I'm concerned, still are, among the very best fiction to come out of northern New England: they are tough, wise, terse; they are violent of deed and lovely of phrase. They are, like the winters in Olmstead's native New Hampshire, fearsome. As was Olmstead himself: with his big red beard and his flannel and his taciturnity, he seemed to me the quintessential northern American writer. Which is to say, he was what I wanted to see, and what I wanted to be. Which is to say, I wanted to be authentic, just like Olmstead.

As everyone knows—well, apparently not *everyone*—you cannot try to be authentic. I mean, you can try, but you will fail. And when you fail, if you are the kind of person I was, you will blame not yourself; instead, you will blame the person you were trying to be.

The first story I handed in to workshop was, I believe, a story about a young man from a dying a mill town in upstate New York (I was from a dying mill town in upstate New York) who wore flannel and who smoked cigarettes and brooded. About what, I don't remember. It might have been about the cigarettes.

About that story, Olmstead said several understatedly unimpressed things that were not untrue.

I sulked and snarked and smoked my way through the rest of the semester. And then Olmstead and I didn't speak to or see each other again for twenty-one years.

YOU WON'T FIND a better book about New England than Olmstead's 1996 memoir *Stay Here with Me*. For instance, this passage:

> New England is still, for the most part, on a hu-
> man scale, which is to say the land does not re-
> quire you to confront it. It is not so blank as to
> make you turn to depend on your mind, not so
> huge that you are dwarfed, not so hospitable that
> you become wasteful, not so brutal that you die.
> But of course it's none of this; it's me remember-
> ing where I was born and raised and where, for
> better or worse, I learned to live.

Everything that is great about the book is in evidence
in this passage: it says a new true thing about a region
so talked about, so mythologized (and self-mythologized)
that you wouldn't think there was a new true thing to be
said about it. In other words, it is authoritative. And then
it undercuts that authority by immediately saying that
this true thing, this brilliant, insightful, authoritative true
thing that has just been said, is in fact entirely personal.
Which is to say, subjective. Which is to say, untrue, or at
least unreliable. Which makes it even more beautiful than
it already was, and it was already plenty beautiful.

Plus, it's very funny. "But of course it's none of this."
That makes me laugh every time.

Stay Here with Me is the book I'm here to praise, but
I fear I've taken an out-of-order approach to doing so.
But maybe that's apt. The passage I've quoted above, for
instance, seems like it should be at the very beginning
of a book. But, in fact, it's at the very end of *Stay Here
with Me*. And this is one of the things I love most about

this book: it is contrary, it cuts against the grain, including the grain of Olmstead's own work. Much of Olmstead's fiction—both the work set in New England and elsewhere—is violent, and that violence—or at least the potential for that violence—makes the fiction unbearably tense, and that tension is ratcheted up by his terrifically taut plotting. But compared to those other books, this—his only memoir—is fond, and positively loose-limbed. It is about the last summer Olmstead spent at his family farm in New Hampshire before heading off to a year of prep school before college. And it is also about a slightly older college student named Afton, a beautiful, mysterious woman who would seem out of Olmstead's league and whom Olmstead of course has fallen in love with. Afton is introduced in the book's beautiful opening scene, and we can already hear the ticking clock on their relationship, and the summer, and Olmstead's life as he's known it.

That would seem book enough.

Except that Olmstead takes every opportunity to write about almost everything else: with the liberal and exhilarating use of flash-forwards, Olmstead tells us about his two friends who help out on the farm and who are headed for dramatically different ends to dramatically different lives; about his father, who does not work on the farm and who is drinking himself to death, which does not cause Olmstead to love him less or write about him less generously; about his mother and grandmother, whose constancy seemingly sets them up to be ignored and underappreciated, except that with his wandering eye and attention Olmstead does not ignore them and does appreciate them; about the farm itself, and the land around it, which Olmstead treats with equal parts fear, hope, boredom, resentment, and wonder; about his cancer-ridden taskmaster of a grandfather, who is one of the grand characters in contemporary American literature and who is the source of much comedy and friction in this book and about whom Olmstead writes, "He enjoyed his mind better than anyone I ever knew." I will never forget that sentence. I know people like that, and you know people like that, but you and I don't know anyone who has described them *in one short sentence* the way Olmstead describes his grandfather.

Which is not to say that the book forgets about Afton. But it is to say that her absences make the reader especially glad to see her reappear. Because when she does, we learn a lot—about her, certainly, but also about Olmstead as a writer. I was shocked when I first read this book. For one, there is enough sex in it to cause the Yankee authorities to tie up Olmstead on the town green and have the citizens stone him with their copies of *Ethan Frome*. For another, Olmstead the character and Olmstead the writer are such kind presences, such good listeners, so curious and open-hearted and -minded—when it comes to Afton, certainly, but really when it comes to *everyone* in this book. And as much as I loved his earlier books— and I did love them and I still do love them, and the later books, too—I did not remember in them those qualities. And I did not remember those qualities in Olmstead's classroom, either.

My point is not that they weren't there. My point is that I was too blindered by my own particular fixations and insecurities and limitations to see them.

No surprise, then, that I have returned to this book several times over the years—with gratitude, the way you do with a book great enough to teach you something about the world, and about yourself, about the writer who made it and about his other books, but also with wonder. And what did *Stay Here with Me* make me wonder? It made me wonder how in the world the Olmstead I knew, or thought I knew, could also be the Olmstead who wrote *Stay Here with Me*.

TWENTY-ONE YEARS AFTER I got a B in Robert Olmstead's introductory fiction class, he invited me to give a reading at Ohio Wesleyan University, where he was then teaching. As I said, we had not spoken in all that time. I was happy Olmstead invited me; I was also nervous. Who knew how we would get along? And for that matter, who knew how Olmstead would feel about my new novel—*An Arsonist's Guide to Writers' Homes in New England*—a book that wasn't exactly reverent about the world he had written about so beautifully.

"Brock was my student, a long time ago," Olmstead said in his introduction to my reading, "and I didn't know what to think about him, and I'm sure he didn't know what to think about me, either."

This sounds ominous, but Olmstead said it sweetly, laughingly and his face, which was now beardless, looked cherubic. There he was, the Olmstead who had written the book in your hands or on your screen. But I still didn't know how he'd done it, or where this Olmstead had come from, until later that night, when I asked Olmstead why he'd shaved his beard, and he said that he was sick of people being scared of him. "People now come up to me in the grocery just to make small talk!" Olmstead said, laughing, obviously so happy. "Strangers!"

Of course, he was the same Olmstead he'd always been. He had just done something different to make you see it.

And that's when I realized what makes this book so different, and why I love it, and why I bet you'll love it, too: *Stay Here with Me* was the book when Olmstead cut off his beard.

Brock Clarke

2024

STAY HERE WITH ME

Me and Afton

GRATEFUL FOR THE breeze, me and Afton climbed Eye Hill, passing through swales of sweet vernal grass and red-top and timothy and bromegrass, plantain and burdock and stalks of mullein on hard, dusty ground, and admired a bull thistle with flower heads as big as my fist and this-tledown long enough to pierce through a finger and took up the Post Road, into the spruce and hemlock and white pine. The air was charged with heat and the countryside was loud with buzzing, with shrill katydids, with cicadas drumming sound on the membranes in their abdomens, and higher up, through the hawthorn and hardwood, the juniper and forest grass gave way to mats of needles and hummocks of green, velvety moss caressing the black earth. Here and there the ground was spongy with the seep of so many mountain springs, to make you think there was a rise of water just off your right hand, high and shaped over with earth and forested with trees, and it was leaking out through the fit of boulders and scrabble of roots—to strike with a stick would make streams to flood.

We followed the Post Road, now come to be just a stitch of path in the forest, tracing round the lay of hills, now quiet and untraveled. In sustained moments, deer flies inflicted themselves, took swats, and kept coming, one by one, until I cut a switch to stir the air around our heads and we passed from their haunts to others.

We crossed stone culverts, caved and sunken, and in some places the water trickled not through them but over them, panning out sparkles and flecks and dapples and stipples shot with light. The smooth rocks were gray and white and orange and blue and glassy, and the mica shown in the lambent light of the late day, lustrous, effortless light, deep with motes of dust, deep with earth cooling and returning its store of heat. The smell of pine was resinous, like camphor in the lucent air, and Afton, with silver rings on every finger and bracelets and beads and her ears pierced twice, was walking the ground the way light would walk if it could, Afton as ethereal as pears.

The Post Road was old and grown in. The sinuous stone walls running its sides had long since gone tumble-down, and inside the walls were trees three-foot thick at the butt—beech and elm and red oak and wild apple had sprawled from orchards, seeding the ground to both sides of the walls, and cherry trees, too, black and angular, and there were stands of trembling aspen, and as we felt the wind on our faces, as it quaked the disklet leaves and off Eye Hill, back at the barn, it moved the vane.

Years later I would come back here with a rifle. Afton will be in New York or Pennsylvania, maybe Salt Lake or Atlanta or Italy. It will be November, early morning and in this very place. At the moment the sun is lighting the melt and snow and the dripping cylinders of ice encasing the stems and twigs and branches of those aspen, a deer will rise up before me, roused from its just lying down, and there will be held in that rising moment all the color my eyes have ever seen, given back to me by the sun through water and bedded in ice. The deer will hightail it across my vision and be out of the territory before I can raise my arms to sight to aim, even if I could raise my arms.

But this was high summer, years before and late in the day when me and Afton started up Eye Hill, stopped awhile to watch a squirrel stutter-run along the top log of a rotted crib for skidding timber, watched it run as if it were jumping through itself, its tail floating behind, acorns and seeds and pods and nuts on its mind. Afton was two years older than me. I was eighteen and she was twenty and I was so in love that, when we touched, my bones ached to come through my skin to meet hers.

Afton liked to think and was a kind of beautiful. She was in love with ideas and books, and sometimes her eyes would flare and she'd go quiet and then patiently explain her thinking. She wore a tan that looked dusted on and she had long white hair and she'd braid it and it'd stay without a clip or barrette for the longest time, slowly coming undone, and then she'd braid it again. One day she was stopped on the street and offered a thousand dollars for her hair and she laughed and shook her head. I know this because I was walking with her. When we walked we fit, and sometimes she'd turn her cheek to my neck and I'd feel like I was king of the universe and she was the polestar and we were in concert.

That was how I was in love with her, but at the time I don't think she'd quite made up her mind about loving me.

Afton had been away from here for some weeks but surprised me when she showed up this sunstruck afternoon. She dropped her yellow Schwinn ten-speed in the grass at lane's end and came walking across the mowing like she'd walked all the way from the seacoast where she'd been.

She said, Hey boy, you been hard at it?

Those were her first words to me this afternoon, and she told me she'd been thinking them up all the way from Newport. Me and Billy were riding the hay wagon. We were shirtless and arm sore, our skin burned umber with sun and exhaust of diesel fuel, and we saw her coming, watched her make that walk in the deadweight afternoon, an electric storm hovering overhead and our hair on end and low down, and mostly under his breath, Billy says, Ever since I can remember that's the dream I've had, to see some woman come walking up out of the earth like that.

He said it like it confirmed in his head that she was Adam's rib, or even like it was woman who came first, made from clay, and then the woman sprang a rib and a spindly little man came to be. Billy said it like it was a reason to live.

Afton brought me a pocketful of shells and stones she'd found on the beach, one for each day she was gone, collected them in her rolled-up shirt, picked them up and would say, Oh, he'll like this one . . . and this one, and each was special in its way.

Said, This one is a scallop and this one is a periwinkle and this one is a dove and this one a whelk and these are all pretty stones. This one is round and this one is flat, this one blue and this red and this white. Said she didn't get in the ocean much because there was a red tide and nobody knew what it was and it was all anybody could talk about down where the water met the land.

The old man saw her coming too, and he stopped the tractor to watch. He was in his heaven up there atop the big blue Ford, towing the baler and hay wagon, making hay come out the chute for me and Billy to hook and stack eight tiers high and, from there, pyramid to the top to send to the barn so the crew up there could fill the halls and aeries of the lofts.

The old man climbed down off the blue tractor and said, How are you, Afton, said it shy like a boy. Said, Those are some nice shells you got there, and then cranked the tighteners to pack another ten pounds into each bale. Afton came aboard the hay wagon as we were finishing the load and then climbed onto the empty one when we picked it up, and she rode with us the rest of the day, more pleased to be on a dusty hay wagon in August than a body should.

Myself, I had never been to the ocean, and it was on the growing list of places I wanted to visit before I died. Not just visit but be a part of; my idea of visiting the ocean was to be a sailor, and my idea of visiting Alaska was to work the pipeline, and my idea of Africa was to hunt and guide and explore, and my idea of Texas was to die at the Alamo, and my idea of Paris was to be in a room and write all this down.

The room would be high-ceilinged and cold in the winter, and when I wrote, I'd wear gloves with the fingers cut back and there'd be a balcony with enough room for a kitchen chair and with a black wrought-iron rail where I could rest my arms in the evening and say things in French to all the fine French people I knew passing by on the cobblestones under the globes of watery, intersecting yellow light. They'd call me by my name, call me down, and we'd drink wine and strong coffee and eat bread and say smart and high-minded things in many languages.

Maybe I'd die in Paris, and people back home wouldn't hear about it until years later. They'd cry and say, That's what he wanted. That's how we knew it'd be. Maybe the French would give me a medal or build a modest statue of me or name a little park after me. Afton said, Street, they name streets after people, and I told her a street with some flowers and a few trees would be just fine.

After a mile it came twilight in those woods on the Post Road, the hushed hour between day and night, and got me to wonder about the lives of the people before electricity: gaslight people, whale-oil people, candle people, the people before the sun decided on its affection for the earth, the lives of the people before they stood on two legs.

Sometimes I think we are forever closed to such wonders. Our minds lead us as far as they will, and most often we discover only our own limitations. We discover only what can be known, discover only what we already know, like what it is to not care when you care, what it is to not be angry when you are angry, to not be sad when you are sad. Our past is always our future, and we build it to be just so, taking pains not to learn, for how frightening that can be. As Afton used to say, It's like trying to imagine what stupid people must think about; it's like what you know is always better than what you don't know, what you like is always better than what you don't like.

"Race you to the top," she said and started running.

I didn't want to run. I'd laid hands on a thousand bales of hay that day, ten thousand in two weeks, touched every one, muscled each into one place or another, my fingers held curled to the grip of a hay hook, and I felt about as strong as a cucumber. But I ran anyway, following behind her, content to see what was ambling before me. Afton ran hard, worked at running, but still ran like a girl, all legs, hips, rolling and tossing her head to feel her hair as horses do when they run.

She stopped to wait, and when I caught up she was bent at the waist with her hair thrown over her head, running her fingers through it.

"Horse flies," she said from under her hair. "Were you watching my ass?"

"Yeah," I said. "I guess I was."

"Help me," she said, and I untangled her hair and wiped the cool sweat from the back of her neck and could not help but kiss her there.

She stood and let her hair fall down and we held each other for a small moment and she said, "Let's go," and we were on the move again.

We cut off the Post Road and huffed up the last steep hundred yards, leaning into the hill, our hands touching down, ready to catch us if we tripped. Up there it was still light, and the summit was a bare crown wreathed in juniper spilling from the ground. This was the meeting place, where there was nothing except grass and sky and a look that went for miles and miles, the forever place, the place I ran to when I ran away from home for an hour.

Billy and Tucker were already there. They'd come up the back side on their motorcycles, the kind of bikes we all had then, bored out, straight pipes, half street and half trail, loud and borderline legal. Billy and Tucker had a couple joints, had collected up wood and started a fire, and there was food and Utica Club beer close by, always close by with Billy and Tucker since a beer truck overturned on Route 12 as they happened by in Tucker's van. A nurse en route to her job at the hospital happened by, too, administered first aid, and then they loaded the driver into her backseat. When she pulled away, Billy and Tucker stood at the roadside, tortured not for long by their solemn oath, Yessir, we will watch that beer as if it were our own.

Alone with the cracked-open beer truck, Tucker turned to Billy, still waving good-bye, and said, You know, sometimes a boy just gets lucky. They ended up with a mountain of beer stashed in the woods under a tarp, well enough for summer into fall.

This was to be a going-away party. Billy and Tucker were getting ready to go to Montana to see all the little towns on the way up the Glacier, where they'd spend out the rest of August, maybe their lives—Rock Creek, Nine Pipes, Shotoe, Blackfoot, Bonner, Big Hole, Bitterroot. They used words like *territory* and said *big sky* and *grizzly bear* a lot, called it a *grizz*, and because they were going and because Billy carried a Montana road map everywhere he went, they seemed to have the right.

Then again, maybe they'd go to Florida, down to the Keys to see the sunset. They hadn't decided. They only knew they'd signed on to get the hay in, and after that they were lighting out, had plans of quitting this part of the country and not ever coming back, plans of going someplace where life was booming.

These were the days when people were up and wandering the country. Some with reason and some without, some looking to shed lives and some looking for new lives, and some just out to flatter their spirits. We all had brothers older than we were, facing the draft, and that weighed and unweighed our own living, gave us reason to think big while we still had a chance, brought home to us matters of consequence, because we knew that, unless things changed, our numbers were up and we'd soon be next.

Afton had been to Montana. She sent me the Montana fishing regulations and a brochure from the Big Hole National Battlefield, which I copied over into a report for my history class and for which I received an A+. My teacher said he really felt like he was there. He said, Thoroughly researched and vivid, highly dramatic and riveting, and some other such shit.

She sent me postcards, too, of another place I'd like to visit, St. Ignatius Mission in St. Ignatius, Montana. I'd have written my report on the mission, but there is just so much information you can copy from off the back of postcards, like the mission was established in 1854 by Jesuits and the Mission Range forms a majestic backdrop and the murals were painted by Br. J. Carignano at the turn of the century. A triptych painted by Carignano depicts the three visions of St. Ignatius, the founder of the Society of Jesus . . . and there was the Lord's Mother in white buckskins, and some guy called the Salish Lord in a headdress.

One way or another, I remember it all. I commit it to memory or copy it down. I collect it up in boxes and envelopes or paste it into a book of blank pages. Any way I can, I remember everything I want to remember.

Afton came and went like that, traveled the compass. She grew up in New York State and New Jersey and as a child attended thirteen different schools, three in the third grade alone, because her father moved around for the fuel oil business. She went to college in Oswego, New York, and her parents lived lately in Newport, Rhode Island.

Although Afton was not from New Hampshire, she had spent the last summer nearby on the lake with her grandmother, who'd been dying for almost ten years, and then she came back. She had been to the lake before, but I didn't know her then.

Afton told me her grandmother had cataracts and arthritis. She was incontinent and deaf and was slowly losing her mind, like it was seeping away, her mind leaking out of her head onto the pillow at night while she slept, and it must be so because each morning she remembered less and less.

"Okay, man, here's one," Tucker said. "Is most of the building on the inside or the outside?"

In one hand he cupped a lit joint and in the other he held a stick, a hot dog skewered on the end, dangling over the flames. He had a beer can open, held between his knees, and another one he'd forgotten about. Tucker was rich in beer and somewhat profligate.

I said, "Depends on how you look at it," and ran a sharpened stick through a hot dog for myself, then for Afton.

"Who cares," she said. "It's something that can be known. You can figure it out. Who cares about something you can figure out?"

"I don't get you," Billy said.

"Easy," she told him. "If it's something people can figure out, like a puzzle or a problem, then what you know can be known by everybody else and what's the point? Like the times tables. What's the point of knowing them? Somebody else already knows. Just ask them."

"Okay, I think I get it," he said, but she vexed him to no end. Billy was a whiz in math, had taken calculus, was mechanically inclined. Where he and Tucker lived, he used magnets to make the electric meter slow down. He had ways to beat the phone company too. He'd do that, and Tucker would watch him and egg him on, all the while eating a bowl of whipped cream, having a beer, and calling it dinner.

I told them the news I was holding, how they could not go to Montana just yet, told them the old man still needed them. He had something up his sleeve and needed their help. They wanted to know what it was, but I only shrugged and said I didn't know.

"Yes, you do. You're just not telling," Tucker said, stuffing a charred hot dog into his mouth.

"Of course he knows," Afton said. "Maybe he's not supposed to tell. Can't you let him keep a secret, at least one?"

"No," they said.

"Okay. He wants to have an aerial photograph of the farm taken and wants you to stay on and help clean up around the place so the picture comes out nice."

"Who's going to take the picture?" Tucker said, passing the joint.

"Afton can take it," Billy said. "Afton can fly into the sky and take the picture."

"I could," Afton said, staring off into the coming night. "Only thing is, I don't know much about cameras. You know, Billy, you give new meaning to the phrase *dull wonder.*"

"Don't be a bitch," Billy said.

"I'm sorry," she said, and I thought she was going to cry. She made a gesture with her hands that meant, Sometimes I don't know what I say, I do things I don't understand.

What I told and what I didn't tell were two different things. The old man, my grandfather, my mother's father, had been diagnosed with prostate cancer and it was advanced and soon it was going to kill him. But I was the only one who knew, not Afton, not my mother, not my grandmother, not sisters or brothers, and besides, he didn't officially tell me, because he didn't officially talk to me, not since I'd grown a handsome Fu Manchu mustache and refused to get a haircut. But he told me everything anyway, when nobody was around, figuring, I thought, that it was safe to tell everything to someone you weren't supposed to be talking to. I kept his tellings. I held his secrets the way a priest or doctor would. Later I would discover he'd established such confidences with most everyone he came in touch with, telling the same story or versions of the same story, and his confidences were held close, honored by all.

"I don't know," Tucker said. "We were thinking of going to Scotland."

"Scotland?"

"Yeah," Billy said. "I love a good bagpipe." And then he spat in the fire.

"Look," I said, "take the work and then take your trip. Maybe I can get him to cough up a little extra money."

Tucker spat in the fire, too. He and Billy were my best friends, but the two of them also had their own friendship and I envied them for that. I think it was at best the way I wanted it, and at worst I had no choice about myself being a little bit separate from them, being a little bit detached. It was a way of feeling I was coming into, and I did not mind so much when I could pass through like a ghost, all eyes and ears.

Tucker looked my way, stroked his hands over his head, collected up his hair into a long, wiry ponytail, and let it fall down his back.

"That's sage fucking advice, Robert. Sage fucking advice. Money talks and bullshit walks."

They received two dollars an hour in haying wages. I was signed on for the summer, a hundred dollars a week, big money back then, but a week was a week, as in seven days long, and a day was fourteen hours from beginning to end, unless we were up-country or some heifers broke fence or some other small catastrophe happened to make the day as long as a day.

It's still like that on the farm. It's relentless work and can make you tired and sad, maybe mean and defeated, but it also gives you some rights. It makes a whole lot of concerns seem not so important.

Billy and Tucker agreed to stay on, and if I could squeeze a few extra bucks per hour out of the old man they'd appreciate it. A dollar alone was worth three gallons of gas.

"Good," Afton said. "Now wasn't that easy?"

But she didn't say it like a question, more like, Now the world is right and good and she was thrilled. There were other times, when we were alone, that she'd as quickly go dark and her eyes almost blank and she'd be silent, and when she was that way I'd be pinned in place, like I was a photograph of myself, or a butterfly, or feather, or miscible ingredients she was stirring round to combine what I was. There is so much I can do in this world, but to know behind those eyes is forever closed to me.

On Eye Hill

UP THERE, ON Eye Hill, we could forget tomorrow and settle down and see the day run into night like wet silver. The swarm of mountains rolled out before us in their summer green, summer lime, summer jade blanket. The juniper smelled like gin, and the fire crackled and pine knots flared and whistled and exploded. Already past was the cooling dewfall, and the chilled air was closing in, but not so much so we could see our ghostly breath or feel it in our bones.

This was land a great way-back grandfather of mine owned, land bought for pennies an acre, drumlins and valleys and benches and saddles of land, with water and runs and rises, abrupt and wooded.

The land used to be cleared for pasture at the steep and for tillage where the incline was not so great, and the timber was harvested. It was dozens of fields, now grown over, yet they could still be read by the walls in the deep woods, by tree lines and fencerows and gullies and wild orchards, squared glades of poplar, by a cellar hole of laid-up stone crumbling down, by shards of colored glass and cut nails, by your own ideas of where to site a house, or clear-cut, or burn over, or sink a plow.

For people with ideas and need, the time and place are always the same. It doesn't matter where you are or when it is. A site for a house or land where things will grow is told to you by the ground and the lay of the sun on that ground, and all you have to do is have your wits about you. Needing to learn something can become the best reason to do nothing in life. You're always waiting around, always afraid to step or speak, afraid to do what people have been doing for thousands of years. The old man used to say, If a man can do it, so can I. Whether true or not, thoughts like that are increasingly my refuge, small acts of willfulness.

This land of Eye Hill was contiguous to the working farm. It ran up the river valley, the long drumlin tapering to my grandfather's house and rising in the direction of the receding ice as it moved north. Seventy thousand years after the ice we sat there, eating and passing round the joint. We drank off the beer, and it cooled us to our skin. Afton ate some bun, and I ate both hot dogs and could have eaten six more, and there were potatoes wrapped in tinfoil nestled in the embers, and we roasted corn and had tomatoes we sprinkled with salt and ate like apples. Billy and Tucker were leaving and I was off to school in Massachusetts in a few weeks. Billy was to have gone to school, too. He was wicked smart and fast, ran cross-country, but needed a scholarship that did not come through to pay his way.

Our bellies full, we lay back in the sleek grass, hands behind our heads, Afton's head on my chest; the pitch of rounded hill afforded us a view down south, down the meander of the river valley, a view of the ice-worn hills, velvety and aqueous with their dense canopy of oak and beech and maple. I could feel the dampness through my T-shirt and blue jeans and it soothed my body as the day's light came under the brow of the evening, soon to be whole dark.

Tucker torched up another joint and we all rolled to be closer, to pass it back and forth. The night was coming, and to our minds and bodies came the lassitude that follows a day of work begun at 4:30 in the morning.

I closed my eyes and held them shut. I stroked a length of Afton's hair, curled it round my fingers. I imagined what I couldn't see: the white bark on those birches I knew to be a mile away, the larine birds sculling the river air that twined the crop ground, the mowings, the bottomland. I imagined the laws of nature, of averages, of motion, of geometry, Moses' law and gravity's law and Newton's law. I thought about what I'd learned from the now-dying old man—you make money buying cows, not selling them; never buy south and sell north; cattle dealers who talk about their families or religion can't be trusted; a cow lives to be eighteen, and a cow should be pregnant or recovering from pregnancy at all times; always work in the direction of home—and I thought about what I'd learned on my own—in spring and fall the ponds turn over; in the summer people don't sleep in bed; when you're struck by lightning, a fern grows in your chest. Afton likes to have her hair combed, is not ticklish, goes barefoot every chance she gets, and sometimes we cannot put a name to our fears, and sometimes people go away and never return.

When I opened my eyes, it was still dark and was August and the stars were punching through in the silent night. The darkness had turned the sweep of land blue and dressy, and a sadness came over me.

"Miles to go," Tucker said. "Miles to go." And he stood and shook himself down, pulled back his hair again. Billy stood, too, and stretched out his fast legs and folded up his map of Montana, thumped it against his thigh.

They said, Tell the old man we're in. Yeah, tell him we're in.

"I'll tell him," I said, and they threw the last of the wood on the fire and kicked up their motorcycles and headed down the drumlin, trumpeting noise, making lights dodge in the air and stab at the trees, and then it went all full silent and stayed that way for the longest time.

In the next few years, Billy would be dead and Tucker would disappear and then show up again, and then he will be dead, too. Before he dies, Tucker will marry and have children and come back to work on the farm for my uncle. Billy will marry, too. He'll marry Carol and they'll have a son, and in a few years, Afton will go to grief because her father will kill himself. These are the things that were waiting for us. These are the things that conspire to break hearts and leave them scarred over.

I sighed and Afton kissed my chest, took her time doing it with love and intent.

"Robert," she said, "do you think about me when I'm gone? It's like I'm always gone."

I lied and said, Only sometimes, and she appreciated that. Whether it was my lying she appreciated or what she took for truth, I don't know which. I didn't tell her about being a boy and crazed by my own self, didn't tell her about how much I thought about her, saw her in every woman and so was desirous of cheerleaders and actresses and field-hockey players and homecoming queens, girls in the band, girls with photographic memories, and girls with no memories at all. In diners I used to write out long poems on place mats and napkins, poems to her, and leave them for the waitress. Once I looked back and saw one reading my napkin, watched her smile and fold it up and put it in the pocket of her smock. I was purely a boy and wanted to ask her the same like question but didn't want to risk the answer.

"It's really none of my business," Afton said. "It's not like we have a claim on each other."

"No," I said. "This seems to be something different, like we are each other's only true company."

"I like that," she said and she repeated it, and then she told me she loved me. She said, "I love you."

"I know you do," I said, telling it as much to myself. "I love you, too. We love each other."

"It's like I bring you to life and you bring me to life."

She trembled in the nightfall and I asked her if she was all right and she said someone must have stepped on her grave because that's what it means when you shiver like that, not a cold shiver but a body shiver.

Afton believed in the afterlife, believed in visiting with the dead, talking to them, inviting them to your home or out on the town, telling them your sorrows and asking them to talk to God on your behalf. She'd say, There are the quick and the dead, the living and the undead.

"I think my grandmother wants to kill herself," she said.

"What makes you think that?"

"She's so morbid."

"That doesn't seem like a good reason."

"What's a good reason?" she said. "People do it all the time. Just last week a man threw himself out his office window twelve stories up, and then two lovers in New Jersey. They parked their car in the garage, closed the doors, and left the engine running."

"Maybe the people in New Jersey, it was an accident. Maybe your grandmother just knows her time is getting near."

I could not imagine such a thing as killing myself. There were people I'd kill for and die for, and I had their names written down in a book and, though that list has become shorter over the years, I still do have a list. But to kill myself was just an idea I'd played around with, same as what would it be like if I could be an animal, what kind would I want to be, or if I had a million bucks, or if I could have one wish. The old man, he got after me when he saw me write stuff down, said, Don't be writing anything down someone can read. Keep it in your head, or don't keep it at all. He'd say, If it's in writing, it's legal.

"Do you think your grandmother will be okay?" I said.

"We better get back. I've been away for all day."

And then we stood and stretched and kissed with our mouths open, and I felt the points of her hips, the slope of her belly, and the drape of her ribs and wished I were willful enough to arrest time and wondered which arm I'd give to do such a thing, and she pulled my head down to her mouth and whispered in my ear.

"Tomorrow night," she said, "call when you're done work and come pick me up. I want to be with you. I want to make love with you, but you can't leave me afterwards. You have to hold me. Maybe you'll want to leave."

"No, I won't," I said. "No, I won't."

"And you'll take me to the fair?" she said, and I told her I would.

We set forth down Eye Hill, night-lit in a fairish glow. We were coming out of the woods, silky and coppery from the gone sun, full of loving-kindness and premonition and superstition, and I heard whisperings, and it was Afton, saying, Everything that is natural is religious, everything that is natural is religious.

The cautious moon presented itself to reflect, to pull tides, to mark time, to be read, to assist birth and betray thieves. The air changed flavor. It gauzed our faces and tasted like almonds, and the atmosphere sparkled and made a nicking sound, like pages turning in a book. I felt as if making love was a secret and we were the only two in the world who knew about it.

"Robert," Afton whispered, "when you become a writer, always write about me. Make me blue and fiery and lunar."

Then we were into the pasture and were amongst the browsing, lowing Holsteins, great ponderous ships of milk, their movements languorous and elegant, like bishops or holy women. They made the pasture hallowed ground.

Farm boys, now old and rheumy with memory, tell stories of following the tanks through pastures in France and Italy. While the guns roared, they caught glimpses of dairy cows grazing in the pastures, lying down to rest, their great angular heads turning, the blink of their liquid eyes. It gave them hope that outside the fences and gates of the death camps, a hundred feet from the wire, the cows blew softly. The fields were plowed and, as thin and tenuous and desperate as it seems, that gave hope, too.

Memory is always more true to the present mind than to the past, always more true to itself than to anything else. This is a story from when I was a kid and worked on the farm for my grandfather and how I see now what I saw then.

A Moment of Fog

IN THE MORNING there was a moment of fog come off the Connecticut River, and I stood in audience.

I watched it rise in a great gray furrow from off the lowest meadow, which I could not see from where I stood on the terrace of land where my mother's family built their big white clapboard house, built the barns and sheds and tenant houses; but I trusted the meadow was there, coursed round by a horseshoe bend and flooded over every spring with snowmelt and rain, rushed over from the ice run, from winter's unlocking door. Left behind would be a bicycle, maybe a galvanized bucket, or a car seat, or tires, or a mattress, and always a tree, bleached gray and bare-limbed, its trunk as thick as a cow's barrel.

The presence of that tree would set the old man off on one of his jags about the old-timey days.

He'd say, We have to clear that field, and I'd say, It's too wet right now, we'd get stuck in the mud. So he'd go up in the attic and find a two-man crosscut saw and a bucksaw and round up some axes and tell one of the men to yoke up whatever team of oxen there was that he hadn't lost patience with and sold or sent to beef.

I'd say, No thanks. If we're going to do this, I'll use the chain saw.

He'd harumph and say, What are you, crazy? It's too wet to use a chain saw.

The old man claimed that wood cut with a bucksaw was warmer wood, and there'd be at least one hired man who'd say, You know, he's right. The old man, he just wanted to yoke up the oxen and see someone break a sweat on a bucksaw. It was because we had a little time on our hands before we could get on the land, and having time on your hands was a bad thing.

The fog bank ascended and I watched it and, for all I know, it was a thousand feet into the sky, but I only cared a little how high. Then it did what it did every morning that summer—it began its roll up the steps of land, over the meadows and the com ground, softly tumbling to where I stood, until it rolled over me and engulfed me and I could feel it on my face, see it bead my arms, and see the beads go to braids and dampen my clothes.

How high? How much time? Those questions seem important only now, only long after and far away. I trust it had height and spent the time it needed. I trust as I trust that falling bodies accelerate at thirty-two feet per second, as I trust there are great lakes underground that might be connected by great flowing rivers that are navigable and that we could sail, and farther down at the earth's core is a furnace, so hot the very imagining of its existence can sear the mind.

I rocked where I stood, feeling the embrace of the river fog come to land. A cow had stepped on my foot that morning while changing directions, and I leaned on that pain. It is a most difficult thing to change the direction of a heavy object. This cow, she knew that much physics and so was hurrying brain messages to her muscles as quickly as she could, because I had begun to whale on her with my cane while yelling and cussing.

That cow, she raised up her head and moaned, pain being what it is and traveling the body more quickly than most sensation. She was trying to squeeze into a place far too small for her wide, lumbering body. She dropped her head and lunged off to the side, and when she heeled like that, my foot became the location of her weight. Now, a cow has a cloven hoof like a sheep, or a goat, or the devil, so when she heeled I could feel her raising up a welt of flesh on the top of my foot, could feel some of those hundreds of tiny bones stressing for position inside my rubber boot, and listened for the sound of something like peanut brittle snapping in my hand.

I rapped her again on the ridge of bone that ran down her back and called her a cross-boned, slack-bagged, evil motherfucker, sang it out to both her ears, and she hied off into another small space, grunting and shouldering aside two of her kind and disappearing into line with two hundred other black-and-white asses. What to do but mutter and limp, find another one to lay into, confess how sometimes these animals were not so beautiful and how I'd often calculated the cost of damage I could do with a revolver and six boxes of shells.

But it was only wishful thinking and it always passed in the time it took to open the lid of the bulk tank and see five tons of white swirling milk and dip out a cup of that milk, or to see a calf born and feed that calf, or to climb aboard a tractor and work the land with plow or disk or harrow, or to plant and mow and bale and chop.

It was like that on the farm. One minute you're hosing down the milk-house floor and the next minute some stray electrical current has knocked you on your ass. One minute you're bending down to set a draw pin and next you realize you've gone and snipped off the end of your little finger. Whether fieldwork or cow work, it always had its dangers, and while the cows made the money, it was the machinery I loved, because it was the machinery that could set me out alone.

Even to this day, when my world seems not so special, there is a winter morning I conjure up. It was some below zero that particular morning, and I was driving the Ford 9000 up off the snowy meadow where I had just spread out a load of cow shit, and in the sky, following after its early light, the curve of the sun made itself apparent on the treed horizon and suddenly the whole universe was there to behold, all diesel fumes and noise and frozen blue mist, and the colors were black and white and green and blue, and each thing looked to not have color but to be color itself, to have color drilled into it. Caught up in the strands of frosted barbwire were lengths of yellowed hair, snagged in the summer from the cows switching their tails, and there I was, all noise and power, making my way through that cold land. This memory delivers me. It is key and conveyance and refuge.

The fog was now past and disappearing up Eye Hill, going ragged in the sun, and I finally allowed myself to think about Afton. Some thoughts you hold back like that. It's like having a small unopened present or a still-sealed envelope. You carry them in your pocket and go to them only when you need to.

The first time Afton called to me like she did the night before, said outright she wanted to be with me, was the winter past, just after the holidays, and I hadn't heard from her much since last summer, the summer we met, and didn't expect to, because she had a college boyfriend. But she'd send me stuff, as I have said, not really letters, but things like a photocopy of her ear that would say, I'm listening, or a copy of her hand that would say, I feel you. Or she'd send me gold leaf, or tiny watercolors, a stone moon, an amethyst, or beads she'd bought in San Francisco off the street, postcards from Montana. One time she wrote me a letter and all it said was, P.S. When we go to Morocco I want to see the people with blue hands.

And then one day last winter, I stopped at the mailbox and found a letter she wrote me and I held that envelope for some days until finally I opened it, and she was telling me she was housesitting for her professor and wanted to be with me, and there was a phone number to call and times when it was good to call.

At first I didn't know where I was, or when it was, or whether I should even call, but I did. I collected enough change to call New York State, so much it was dragging my pants down, and went into the village where there was a pay phone. I dialed the number and put in the coins the operator asked for and then, without its ringing so much as once, she answered a phone three hundred miles away, like she knew it'd be me.

"How have you been?" she said.

"Good," I said.

"What have you been doing?"

I told her I went to see Jefferson Airplane at Keene State College. Billy and Tucker went, too. We sat in the bleachers, got high, and on a big screen they were showing all watery shapes with an overhead projector. Papa John Creach played for a long time and then, about midnight, Grace Slick came out and she was far-gone pregnant, eight months' pregnant, and big as a house.

"I have been very happy lately," she said, "and I would like to see you. I want to be with you." Then there was a long silence and she said, "Why aren't you here?"

"I want to be with you, too," I said, struck warm in that wintry phone booth, telling myself to settle, to settle. "When are you coming back to New Hampshire?" I asked.

"No, you come here," she said, and that's how I came to hitchhike to New York State in February, a place that in my mind might as well have been on the other side of the moon.

I traced my face with that touch of memory. I could see Cy heading my way, shuffling over to where I had witnessed the moment of fog come off the Connecticut River. Lately he'd given up his tall black rubber boots for a pair of Converse sneakers, but he still wore forest-green trousers and faded blue chambray shirts buttoned at the neck. Cy was born old, ninety years old and he'd seen it all. When he was born, Sitting Bull was still alive. According to Cy, he'd had all the babes in two centuries and had intents of laying waste to a third, but over the winter he'd stroked out on the toilet. I was in his kitchen at the time, eating doughnuts and drinking instant.

Cy and his wife, Lila, lived in a tenant house off the far end of the barn, a house held on both ends in the grasp of lilacs. I say the grasp of lilacs because when I was a kid I came out the end of that barn on a tractor, with a few tons of cow shit hooked behind me, and the brakes gave out. More accurately, the tractor was without brakes and the hired men had neglected to tell me. The nigh lilac bush caught me up as I tore through in a spray of twigs and branches and pink blossoms. I'd always been fond of lilacs and so was happy to be saved by one.

The winter Cy stroked, it'd been my habit to slide over to their house in the dark morning and eat Lila's doughnuts. They'd be hot and heavily dusted with powdered sugar, sodden with grease. Lila smoked Pall Malls at the kitchen table all times of the day. There was a yellow smoke stain cast on the ceiling over where she sat, and the hair to the front of her head was stained in that same way. To say she was a big woman would only be a lie. She was huge, the hugest woman I ever knew. She sat with her elbows resting on a slice of foam rubber because her arms

were too heavy for even her. She grew dangerous finger-
nails, and when she moved, she moved the way a glacier
would, moved like a plate in the earth, moved like a season.

In his prestroke days, Cy was a killer. He loved to see
the blood run. I watched him run down critters with a
mowing machine, saw him not flinch when he realized
he'd snicked the legs off a fawn in deep grass with the
cutter bar. There was also the time we had a down cow and
it was fading fast. We dragged her onto the truck and it
looked like she wouldn't live to reach the slaughterhouse,
where they prefer to do their own killing but would sometimes take a cow if she'd just been bled. The old man sent
me into the house for the sharpest knife I could find and
handed it over to Cy, told him to take care of her, told me
that man sure loved to see the blood run.

I'll never forget the delight in his face as he held the
handle of that knife and walked up the tail end, or the
sound of him sawing away, the moan and the flush of
blood when he found what he'd been looking for inside
her neck. Since then I have found my own self on the
handle end of a sticking knife, gutting knife, skinning
knife, boning knife.

When I got my first knife, I thought about honing it
with a whetstone. It was a beautiful knife. It had cost me
some books of S & H Green Stamps I'd pilfered over the
months from my mother and her sisters and my grandmother. I thought what a fine act that would be, the working
of steel and stone there in my hand. So I went to Cy's house
to see about borrowing a whetstone and he said, Nah, you
don't want to waste your time with a whetstone, and took

me into his shed and pulled back a square of tarp revealing a brand-new bench grinder. He hit the switch and held my new knife on the tool rest, eased it into the spinning stone wheel. A flying horsetail of red sparks came from the point where steel and stone met, and billowed out from there.

I watched my new knife heat and change color, saw it glaze and hold the mark of that heat.

I didn't know it, but I was watching the taking of whatever temper my cheap knife held. I know some stuff now about heat and steel and wire edges and angles of sharpening, but still, at the time, it didn't take much to judge the scored blade and the scalloped edge I'd been left with.

There, he said. There's your sharp knife.

Another time, Afton sent me a jackknife. She wrote, I bought this for myself, but because I know you love knives and know how to use them without cutting yourself, I trust it with you. It was as if to say even a small thing can have a mind of its own and, just in case, we are to honor the possibility.

Cy walked right on into me during that rising fog and bounced off, like he was carried not of himself, like he was brushed up on a small wind, not much left of the man who'd had all the babes in two centuries. The prospects didn't look good for a third.

"What the fuck's going on?" he wanted to know, acting like it was me hit him.

He never did so much speak to you as he'd snarl in the direction you were in, and after the stroke he couldn't even do that very well. Slowly his speech was coming back to resemble words, his voice thick and labile. I had come to understand what he was saying, but me and Lila were about the only ones.

"Nothing," I said.

"Something's up."

So I told him how the old man wanted to have an aerial photograph of the farm taken and we were to get everything in apple-pie order.

"What the fuck is that?"

"You know, a picture of the farm taken from the sky. An aerial photograph."

"Big fuckin' deal."

"He wants to get a preview of what it'll look like after he dies."

"Be better off digging the deepest goddamn hole he can and looking up from the underground." Then Cy gave off his idea of a laugh, as if he'd seen his own world from hell, and the laughter caught up in the paralyzed side of his face and looked like it went to pain.

Billy and Tucker showed about that time, pulled up in the VW bus. They made a big show of letting a dozen empty beer cans fall out the doors when they opened them, thought that was funny and so did I.

"Hey, numb nuts," Tucker said. "How's it going?"

"Good," I said. "Real good."

They told me they'd decided they were going to Mexico and that was final and they hoped they'd meet up with a lot of peyote and pretty women and didn't end up in the hoosegow. They were thrilled with their latest final decision and I envied them, wanting to be able to go with them in the worst way.

"We're going to work a couple days and then we're gone," Tucker said.

"A couple days and we are history," Billy said.

"Cy, you're looking real good this morning," Tucker said. "You getting much?"

Cy shuffled a little, toed some cow shit, and almost lost his balance. Cy didn't say anything with other people around, couldn't say much, but I knew he was having those *When I was a younger man, I'd whip your ass* kind of thoughts.

Hell, he'd been buried alive in sawdust, had to paw his way out, and another time he heated an ax head red hot, the same ax he'd injured himself with, and cauterized his leg wound so as to hike out of the woods in the dead of winter. You need to have high regard for people like that, people whose lives are not common or ordinary, the ones who rise up and continue on, the ones who last.

The old man saw us standing there and hustled himself over as if in our moment of idleness we'd go to murdering and pillaging, laying waste to the countryside. He wanted to know if we were going to get to work sometime that year. Then he undid his trousers and reached in to rearrange his balls, like he was scratching his head or something.

"I want this all burned," he said, still holding himself in his hand.

We'd already been through it at breakfast, how he wanted the place cleaned up, neat as a pin. There was brush and rubbish and a summer's worth of sumac, downed limbs and cartons and twine and all such.

"I told you we can just throw it in the gully."

"I want it burned," he said to Tucker, "and, by gawd, don't burn down the place while you're at it."

He wanted fire like sometimes he wanted a baked potato. He'd get it in his head he wanted fried clams and drive two hours for them, or, I should say, get someone to drive him two hours for them, and then the next day he'd snicker about someone else doing the very same foolish thing. When his whim wasn't satisfied there was hell to pay. He wasn't someone who tolerated disappointment. Even his whimsy was driven by willfulness. Today he wanted fire. He wanted the acts and elements of life.

"That picture will be taken sooner than later," he said to Tucker.

"When is sooner than later?" I asked.

"Sunday. It's got to be Sunday," he said to Tucker, like it was Tucker talking and not me.

"What Sunday? This Sunday or next Sunday?"

"The weather is to be good on Sunday for picture taking from the sky."

"Oh."

"Hey," Tucker said, pointing to the drive, "you ought to get the fire department to hose all this down. Blast it all clean and pretty."

The old man looked at him and smiled and then he turned to Cy.

"You coming with me," he said.

I tried to remember if the old man ever asked a question like a question and if he ever asked a question he didn't already know the answer to. Cy grunted and followed out after him.

Since Cy had gotten back on his feet, the old man had let him come back to work, and you'd know he was around by the hushing sound his broom made on the manger floors. Sometimes he'd ride with the old man, up north to buy cows or to one of the pastures we rented, to check on the heifers.

The morning he stroked out I was sitting with Lila, finishing up the doughnuts and trying to talk her into making me a cheesecake. I told her I'd buy all the ingredients. No lie, her cheesecakes weighed about eighty pounds and you could eat off them for a month. I played high school football and was headed to prep school for a year to get ready for college and I wanted to bulk up.

Then we heard a crash and a clatter and a rush of water. It was the sound of a body going down on something hard and that body upsetting other hard things. Lila yelled and whooped, and I lit out to see what was the matter. Cy was laid over on his side, his pants about his ankles and his privates hanging out. There was water everywhere, as he had somehow managed to tear the tank off the back of the toilet. There was no writhing, no uttering of sound, just him staring up at me, his eyes gone vitreous, his legs tucked and his arms askew. No whimper, no cry, just his eyes, blank and glassy, staring up at me, and then I could see coming to his eyes from way off in his head faint pulses of fear that assured me he was still alive, pulses that said, This could be it and I am afraid.

"There goes a couple old crusty bastards," Tucker said.

"Fossils," Billy said.

I told them we were to find whatever rubbish we could, baling twine and sacks and boxes, busted-up snow fence and brush, and there was brush to cut and various junk and pieces of ruined and useless equipment, and we were to haul it all down the back lane and heap it up and burn it and doze it off into the gully. There was mowing that needed to be done. There was painting and sweeping and scything and repairing.

While we worked, other lives were being lived on the farm, other work being carried on. There was an ex-con who was overhauling an engine. There was my uncle, milking and breeding and doctoring cows. There was a farmhand who spent his day in the bunk silo hand loading a dump truck of ensilage. There was young stock to feed and water. There was constant feeding and sweeping and cleaning and handling and shoveling. There were six or eight men at work at all times and two or three strays the old man would bring home from time to time. The old man was always bringing home a new best hired man and setting him up as someone he could boss around.

My mother and aunts and grandmother, they worked, too. They chased cows and sometimes swept and fed. They cooked and cleaned and went to Concord to get blood tested so as to ship cows about the country and kept the books and went to the bank. They were always going to the bank and the grocery store and to church. My girl cousins had summer jobs and rode horses, but my boy cousins were still too young to work. I was watching them grow and getting into trouble with them, and I knew from an early age they'd be the ones to take over the farm someday because I was born to a daughter and not a son. But for now, me and Tucker and Billy were like the old man's private crew on loan to his whims.

We set to work, and after a spell the morning burned off and the day turned even brighter than expected. There was an up-slant light in the air, the kind of light that comes to earth and bounces off whatever it touches, light that finds its way into everything. Where there is chaff in the alleys, it makes walls of that chaff, and where there is water, that water dazzles, and where there is tar, that tar shimmers, and where there is concrete, the aggregate becomes rutilant in the glary light. This is light that glitters and reveals nothing. It was in that light where we worked, shirtless and smudged and dirty from manhandling oil drums and grease buckets, pieces of machinery so cannibalized for parts you wouldn't know what they were unless you'd been there from the start. It was in that light where we cut brush and hauled truckloads down the back road to the edge of a gully under a bluff.

In the wintertime, when I had talked to Afton, I knew it wasn't going to be an easy sort of thing to go gadding off to Oswego, New York. I had never flown or been on a train or a bus, and I had no car of my own. Going to Oswego was an idea out of the ordinary, and my family's hold on the ordinary was tenacious, and for that sometimes we fought terribly, my mother and me and my father and the rest of us. We fought because my father drank too much, and because we didn't have much money and work was always and hard, and because there was anger and some-times for the sport and pleasure of fighting.

It was recreation, and in that water you sank or swam. I held my own, but it was like my skin didn't fit, or my brain was lopsided. I could be mean and angry. I think I came into this world with a temper, and now everything I do is to keep that temper from boiling over. There'd be knockdown drag-outs. My brother and I would play at wrestling or do Three Stooges gags, and my mother would come after us with a barbecue fork, not so much to stop the fight, which she had about given up on, but to chase us out the door to fight on the lawn so we wouldn't break any furniture.

One time we made bows and fashioned arrows out of woody reeds and did battle. He shot me in the mouth, peeling a layer of skin from the roof of it, and he told me we'd better not say anything or we'd get in trouble, and I agreed. Why I thought *we* would get in trouble and not just him was a testament to the life we were in. So he took a pair of scissors and snipped away that skin and told me I'd be all right, and I believed him and I was.

After I got back from that cold phone booth, back from calling Afton, I went down to the basement to think over how I was going to up and go to Oswego. Down in the basement I had a place for myself to think, a ta-ble and a chair I'd set up next to the water pump. I had books and I remember who the writers were: Camus and Freud, Shakespeare, Marcuse, Sartre. They were books given me by my sister's fourth-grade teacher, who liked me. He counseled my father and sponsored him at AA meetings and took pleasure in challenging my woeful ignorance. He thought there was hope for me. I looked at those books. I'd been reading them for some time and didn't understand much they were saying but trusted they were important because they had a way of saying things seriously.

I collected a stack of those books and rested my head on them. What I could do was start a fight with my mother and go storming out of the house. It worked like this:

"Is that spinach?" my brother would say.

"No, it's Swiss chard," my mother would say. "With spinach you get the little beets on the end of it. It's not spinach; it's Swiss chard."

"What do you think it is?" my brother would ask my father, who would not put down his newspaper, would not look at the vegetable in question.

"Looks like rhubarb to me," he'd say from behind his newspaper.

"So Catholics and Jews won't go to heaven," I'd say.

"No," she'd say.

"Will unbaptized babies?"

"No."

"What'd they ever do to anyone?"

"They weren't baptized."

"Will animals?"

"No."

"What about dogs? Dogs seem okay."

"No."

"What about cows? You always see pictures of God leaning on a cow. People in heaven will need milk."

"What kind of cows?"

"Brown Swiss."

"No."

"Well none of that seems fair, especially about the babies and the Jews and Catholics."

"Do you think I like it any better than you do? You have to believe that all things work to the good of all things."

"Then there is no bad?"

"Well, it isn't all good."

At some point in here voices would rise and what began as sport would become a small war.

I could have done that this time, but I didn't. Instead, I began to think about the skier who crossed the property two, three, four times a day that winter. I'd seen him the night before, a speck against the mountains that rose up beyond the river in Vermont. I knew who he was. He lived alone and was training for the Olympics. I'd watch him from the platform at the milkhouse door, which was elevated eight feet above the road so that when Mr. Parker came for the milk, gravity's pull would do the work of loading his tanker.

I'd watch the skier make his pass across our land, his arms sawing the air and his legs sweeping over the snow. From where I was I could hear no sound except the sound of stanchion chains, the gushing of water in the drinking bowls, the groan and stretch of cows standing and lying down.

Or I'd see him from the barn roof, where I'd been sent to shovel away four feet of snow burden. He'd be passing through the snow plumes way off, and I'd be surrounded by the snow smoke coming off the peak, and for a moment he'd make m feel as if we were the only two people alive in the world.

I'd seen him that night, seen him and wanted to be as unnoticed, so the next morning I packed a knapsack and just up and said I wasn't going to school that day but instead was going to Oswego to see Afton. I asked for a ride to the interstate.

My mother said I wasn't going.

My father said, Listen to your mother.

My brother said he'd give me a ride to the interstate and grabbed the keys to his truck. A little while later, when he let me out, he said, You know, and don't take this the wrong way, but things are a lot quieter when you're not around.

I knew my brother to be sincere and to not be someone who trafficked in what was beyond the obvious or the admitted. No offense was taken, and I had to say that I already suspected as much.

Oswego

HITCHHIKING TO OSWEGO was wishful travel.

It was a harsh winter, and I have traveled in the unbeautiful since and seen it to be such, but the way to Oswego had all the charm of conveyance without mechanism, something soulful without intermediary. It wasn't long before I was farther from home than I'd ever been in my life. The way was easier than I thought it would be. I met an artist who said he'd paint my picture and send it to me, so I wrote down my address. He asked me how I'd be if he wanted to give me a blow job, and I told him he could let me out, but he said not to panic. He'd take me as far as he was going. When I did get out I told him he was a sick fuck and slammed his door as hard as I could.

Afton told me later I should have taken it as a compliment. The guy found me attractive was all. It was a new way of thinking for me, but let's just say I didn't plunge on

44

into understanding and relief at that moment. I'd take my time about doing that.

In Albany I hooked up with a black guy and we caught a ride on to Syracuse. He told me he'd hitched all over the world, but he was without a coat and wore loafers with no socks, so I gave him my poncho. He was grateful and asked for my address and said he'd mail it back, but he never did.

I didn't know what I was looking for in Oswego. Yes I do. I was looking for someone, her, where life could be all different. I was looking for her to take my sad boy heart and heal it, give me something in the world that I could draw on for strength and courage and miracle from time to time. I believed in such things as Lazarus coming back from the dead, Moses parting the Red Sea waters, and that water could be made into wine and fishes, and loaves of bread could be made to multiply to feed the people. Even now I half believe everything I am told and believe a little bit those things I know to be not true, in case I am wrong.

In town I found the address, and she took me in her arms and was all warm and soft. It was our second holding. Our first was the summer before, when we weren't supposed to be holding because she had a college boyfriend. We kissed then, too, a long, shy kiss that was more the touching of mouths. She walked me through the rooms silently, me not knowing how to behave. It was a nice house. There was a couch. There was a stereo system I bent down to look at as if I knew something about stereos. There were fragments of embroidery and framed quilt blocks. There was a lot of woodwork, blond and slender.

This was someone's house and they were gone and we were there. There was not a familiar piece of furniture, not a rug, not a painting, not a photograph I'd know, not a familiar coat left draped over the newel post. It was a woman's house, for sure. There was a woman's smell and there were living things and dried things. There was potpourri, cinnamon, and rose and hyssop. There was ficus, a Boston fem, bridal veil, and a wandering Jew. Afton told me that it was a woman's house because in the spice rack there was saffron.

Afton told me these things while, inside, tides of emotion were running through me. Should we talk about me being there? What should we say? What will being here be like? Maybe I should tell a joke. Afton sat in a chair and picked up a pen, and I found a space of wall where I could lean.

"Get something to eat," she said. "You must be starved."

"That would be nice," I said. "I'm famished."

"That's such a pretty word, *famished*."

"Yes, it is."

"There's a kind of totalness about it. I think I'm going to take a shower and put on some clean clothes," she said.

She set down her pen as quietly as possible. She'd been doodling on a pad by the phone. She'd been drawing what are called chaotic harmonies, chaotic flows. Her pen had been orbiting the center. She'd left a space and made a stick figure there.

"Sounds like a good idea," she said, standing and sighing, not remembering it was her own. She sighed again and said, "Well, okay."

Then she picked up my knapsack and went upstairs to the bathroom and I followed, followed her right into that bathroom. Not until I got in there did I realize what I'd done and how it might not have been the thing to do, but she didn't say anything. She seemed as amazed as I was but didn't say anything.

She made the spray hot and took off her clothes and stepped over the tub wall, and as those clothes came off I felt like the floor was swallowing me up again and again. She asked me if I wanted to come in, too, and so I took my clothes off and stepped into the pins of water, and it was like a narcotic.

"See," she said, *"Couple,* by Matisse."

It had been painted on the shower wall, two people holding each other. She swayed under them, telling me how she could feel her aches going to tiredness. She held her hands to her chest and told me she'd been thinking about this, just like this.

"Your turn," she said, stepping aside so I could get under the water.

"Is your professor an artist?"

"Turn around," she said and took up the soap and washed my back and told me I had a vast back. "Art history," she said.

When we passed under the water again, we touched and we kissed and we didn't stop touching, didn't stop being near to touch, didn't stop knowing each other, ever again.

That night we ate at a restaurant in town among people who were strangers to me. In small moments, I'd remember her naked body before the shower and in the shower and after the shower, and my breath would go away and I'd have to squeeze the edge of the table or push my foot hard against the floor.

I liked how she was as apt to take food with her fingers as with her fork. She'd say, Here, taste this, and she'd feed me. I liked that, and then, out of the blue, with her mouth full, she'd start talking about what an asshole Nixon was and about the injustices in the world. A war gets fought in all manner of places.

Another couple came into the restaurant. Right away I could tell he was her old boyfriend, and she confirmed it and told me they'd almost been engaged but now it was over.

"It was just a college love," she said.

I didn't say anything. I pushed at the food on my plate and she did the same with hers.

She let her shoe slip off her foot and got her toes on my shin. The point of contact moved up my leg. I wondered if that was why she called me, because this breaking up had been a recent event.

Then there was this new old thing rising between us inside our skin. It was her foot like a hand on my leg, and for a second I wanted to ask her if she'd ever done that before with him, but then I hated what thoughts my brain could deliver.

"You know," she said, "when you were on your way, I had the most horrible thought that you'd be hurt. My God, that would have been awful."

She had made herself sad by her fears. She went all quiet and dark around the eyes and I thought she might cry.

"No," I whispered. "I was okay."

"Shall we walk off this meal?" she said.

"Yes. Let us," I said. "Delightful," I said, and that made her smile. I didn't know anybody who said words like *shall* or *delightful*, but I was enjoying this. She nodded and began to collect herself, glanced at the bill and left some cash. She told me it was her treat.

Outside, the night was cold. She took my arm and didn't let go. After a block, her other hand was up and holding my arm, and then we had our arms around each other and we walked that way and I could feel how warm her bones were down through those sweaters and coats.

We walked down by the lake, Lake Ontario, and it was a difficult thing for me to fit inside my brain. It was gray and moonstruck and frozen, great buckles of ice heaved up into the sky, and strange, too, how it seemed at rest, like whatever happened had come and gone and left the lake the way it was that night for us to see, endless and impossible to cross. A wind was coming from the north, down from the top of the earth, and she told me that sometimes that wind could pick up and sweep you off your feet, sometimes students ventured onto the ice and were never seen again.

We walked onto the campus and into the student union for doughnuts and hot chocolate. We held hands, and there were a lot of people who waved to her and said hello and there was music, and after a while the guy from the restaurant came there, too. He came up to Afton and started talking to her. He was whip-thin, had a goatee, and wore a big shirt all daubed with paint, like artists wear. He was close to her ear, saying things I could not hear because of the music, but I could tell they weren't nice things by the look on her face and the way she folded into herself.

I thought, He's hurting her with what he's saying and I can take this guy and it wouldn't matter anyway, because I won't let anybody hurt her. My next thought was, I am so far from home.

"Fly, Afton. Fly," he yelled, and then he laughed.

I want to say I punched that whippy guy in the head,

did one of those things where you drive a guy's nose up into his brain and kill him instantly and the jury finds it all old-fashioned and chivalrous and I am the hero, but I didn't do anything. I stood there like a dope, and strangely enough Afton thanked me for not getting involved.

I have had something explained to me since, by Afton and others, and have explained it to others myself, as if I knew what I was talking about. It seems that sometimes it's okay to be helped. Sometimes it's okay to fall to pieces in not any common way and let someone help you out.

Afton licked her finger and put it in my ear and I felt it down through my body. She kissed me, and then we were kissing each other and people around us were watching. I pulled at her fingers like they were taffy.

"Thanks for not duking him out," she whispered.

"What makes you think I was going to do that?" I asked.

"Because you are an open book. Let's get the fuck out of here," she said in her best movie voice. "Let's blow this pop stand."

We walked back to the house she was taking care of. The air was crisp, gone sharp cold, and I could taste it in my mouth. Then we were in the house, in the bedroom, and she was barefoot, like summer, and the first thing she did was make my feet bare and take one in her hands and massage it. Then she did the other one, kissing them both.

She stroked my forearm. I got up and stood at the foot of the bed and looked at her. The bedroom was white and without light, was dark and shadowless. I didn't know what I was doing just standing there. I wanted to say something beautiful about hearts and souls and spirits and destiny, wanted to make a speech about love, wanted to stop time so this moment would never end, but I didn't.

I reached to unbutton my shirt, and she said, "No, let me do that." She slid down to sit at the foot of the bed. Her own shirt parted and I could see she was naked underneath. She looked down at herself. She looked up at me and smiled.

"I think I'd feel better if we kissed some more," she said, and I was all for that. That was enough for both of us because those kisses came from the same place where pain and hunger live.

Then she lit candles. They surrounded the bed, illuminated the dresser, the spines of books. She lit cinnamon candles and we lay on our sides, face to face. I could hear car engines outside. I could hear voices. I could hear doors opening and closing, could hear these candles sputter and gutter. I had never been in a bedroom where I could hear the voices of strangers.

She got out of bed and put a robe on over her clothes. She lit a cigarette, her first in a long time, she said, and walked about the room, taking puffs and then, with the back of her hand, waving away the smoke she exhaled. She looked for an ashtray but couldn't find one, so she tapped her ashes into a jade plant and I watched her, said her name, felt as if I'd been watching her all this life, wanting her to be mine and have her want just that. I wondered how foolish I was being. She sat down in the armchair close beside the bed, her feet up and tucked into my side, and I fell asleep for a while.

Then the phone was ringing in the night, waking me, and she was beside me in bed, in my arms.

"Don't answer it," she whispered, and I didn't, had no intention of answering it.

I rolled to the edge and let one foot down onto the floor. I sent all my weight and strength into that foot. I tried to spike the floor to the earth. I got out of bed and treated myself to a drink of water and a cigarette. I sat by the window, the curtain turned back enough so as to afford the room a sliver of light. The street lights floated in the night, suspended in the misty air. There was no traffic now, no noise that entered the room. A block away, a red strobe worked the darkness; some life was in emergency. I sniffed at the cigarette smoke, imagined the smell of a burning house.

Out beyond, where I could not see, was that lake, and I wanted to be at the edge of it again until I understood it. I wanted to get bundled up and sit there on a rock, as if I were the first to come across it and my thoughts were the first thoughts to travel over it.

I stubbed out the cigarette in the jade plant and got another glass of water from the bathroom sink. In the darkness I turned left instead of right outside the bathroom door and wandered the upstairs, ending up in a room to the north. There was the smell of paint thinner and linseed oil. I found a switch, and blinding light poured in from the ceiling and the corners. The room was bigger than I had imagined in the dark. There was a wall of books, an easel with a primed canvas, and brushes, palettes, knives, glazes, varnishes, and paints, all clean, unopened, dry, neatly arranged.

Alone, possessing its own wall, was the painting of a woman back on her elbows, her knees up, a seashell on her stomach. I stared at the painting until I heard Afton calling my name, and I made my way back to her.

I remember catching sleep those nights, and she remembered the phone ringing in the darkness but wasn't sure. It was the first time I'd ever slept with a woman, and her smell was on my hands, the feel of her slick thighs, her skin cool, almost cold, between her legs. We weren't able to get much beyond kissing and touching for fear of melting or exploding. Kissing was enough to bear.

We did other things, too. We saw a play—*Spoon River Anthology*—and a dance performance, and, one night, there was a warming and a dorm lit up like a Christmas tree. A student came onto a balcony and shot bottle rockets, calling out to the other students, and a whole pageant began. People came out of nowhere dressed up like the twelve disciples, the seven vestal virgins, kings and queens and dancers, people on horseback, jugglers, unicyclists, dogs with neckerchiefs. Kegs of beer materialized and joints were being passed around. There were people on stilts, and singers and guitars, and still more people came, all in winter in the snow, nobody cold or sad.

The next day there were flowers in the student union for students to buy for one another and put in mailboxes. That night we lay in bed holding each other, sad because I was leaving in the morning. I held her tightly, held her to my chest and told her I did not want to go, and she said I had to.

"I am so in love with you," I said to her. "I feel like I am coming apart."

"You have to heal yourself," she said, touching my face, and there came to me a fleeting and frightening moment when I didn't like her for having told me that. Heal myself? I wanted to say; I have unstitched myself because of you, because of your being, and you tell me to heal myself. Don't tell me that. But I knew I had no hold on her, could make no demands, no requests.

I thought to say, Pretend I'm just nobody, looking for a small handout; to say, Lie to me, tell me anything and we'll agree you're lying—just do it so I can take the words with me. I settled down on the bed on my stomach, all boyish and sad. On the floor next to the bed was a pink plastic watering can, and I took it in my hands and squeezed it until it snapped and snapped again, and each time it snapped she made a sound of fear and surprise, and then it came apart and water rinsed out the fissured plastic to puddle on the floor.

That night we entered half sleep, the sleep haunted by dream and thought and movement and memory. We spent the night fleeing out of sleep, close to touching but paralyzed by not knowing what was between us. In the morning she said to me, "It isn't like we are sunny people who can be all cheerful and lighthearted."

"Are there such people?" I asked, and the look on her face told me she didn't know.

"I'll make us some coffee," she said. "Maybe there's something to eat."

We drank coffee, and then we hugged and I hitched on out of there, wondering about the road, about danger, about dying, about the long haul back to New Hampshire.

I wasn't afraid, because she and that lake were over my shoulder, like they were the edge of the world and that's where I'd been.

Out there was only me and strangers and a strange land to pass through, and I drew strength. I had good luck and found myself, late that morning, outside a tollbooth in Syracuse, in a driving winter rain, and even that was okay until a state trooper stopped and called me into his car. He reached over to frisk me, asked about drugs and knives and concealed weapons and cash. I was polite and he told me I wasn't to be hitchhiking on the thruway, so he drove past the tollbooth and let me out on the other side, told me to watch myself and stay out of trouble.

I wanted to tell him he was the only trouble I'd run into. I wanted out of there and would take any ride, so I began hitching both directions. A young guy coming out of the tollbooth picked me up. Where you going, he asked, and I said I didn't know or care. I didn't have much money. He told me I could panhandle at the bus station, so he dropped me there. I called home.

My mother answered and I told her I was in Syracuse, at the bus station.

She said, Don't go anywhere, and hung up.

I sat in the bus station, content to not move, as my mother told me. I wasn't anywhere anyway, and it didn't matter to me. I was coming off the biggest trip of my life. I was wet but getting dry. I was cold but warming up. I watched people arrive and depart.

I thought about how it is to see someone off on a train, or plane, or bus. I watched couples part and unite and felt a bit of their sadness and joy each time, and, as much as I wanted it to, my mind would not let me leave Afton.

Nursing a coffee, I watched two people my own age. I watched them kiss, saw her hand on his neck, saw his hand go for a last touch of intimate flesh at her waist, between her sweater and her belt, inside her coat, and I was both of them. I felt myself sinking into them.

I thought to stop loving, because I didn't want to be them, not ever, but I knew I couldn't help myself. I would forever be not so much my own self as like something that gauges wind or heat or cold, something that contains within it a rising and falling, a turning and a measuring.

I saw a young woman in high-heel shoes. They were red and shiny, like blood or the insides of an animal, and she walked right up to me and said my name.

"Yes," I said, and she told me she was the secretary at a Lutheran church in Syracuse and that my mother had called. She gave me bus fare back to New Hampshire.

"You should go straight home," she said. "Your father is in the hospital."

"What is it?"

"Your mother didn't say but said to tell you it was serious and to come home as soon as you can."

"Thank you," I said.

"You're welcome," she said, and then she smiled and told me I had a very handsome mustache. "Your mother said it's how I was to recognize you."

My Own Father

WHEN I WAS a child it was always nighttime, my mother waiting at the window for my father to get home from the factory, and it was always winter, always cold and wet, the room lit by the moonlight banking off the snowfields and coming through the picture window and the room lit by a flickering black-and-white Zenith television set, constantly in need of vertical hold. Some nights the headlights would be my mother's father, come by in a truck to pick up me and my brother and take us to my uncle's farm in Walpole. He'd back onto the barn floor and send us up into the black hayloft to feel our way, to undo the summer's work and send down bales of hay to load on the truck. They would feed the heifers that wintered outdoors along an icy brook that flowed to the Connecticut River.

Sometime in there, my father would show up to eat his supper and drink his Black Label beer and fall asleep.

We'd get back a few hours later to do our homework, a five-dollar bill to split between us.

My father was a good man. He built me a big toy box out of yellow pine and shellacked it to be smooth and shiny and the pine more yellow. He glued felt to the bottom and hinged the lid with a chain so it couldn't fall back, and he painted my name on the front, built one just like it for my brother, too. At night, on weekends, he fished for horned pout in the reclaim ponds by the light of a lantern, and on rare Saturday mornings took my brother and me down to the river to catch whatever came along—perch and pike and trout and fat-lipped bony carp.

He liked to build dams in the little streams and watch them break and the water flood, and he'd explain how that worked on the grand scale of things. One time he built a waterwheel. We took it down to the brook and made a sluiceway and watched it spin, and he explained that, too. He gave me advice like: Better to keep your mouth shut and let the world think you're a fool than to open it and let everyone know, and one time, when I said the word *nigger*, he slapped me so hard I saw stars.

My father worked in Keene. He started out on the shipping floor in the factory and worked his way up to an office job. He knew everything there was to know about bolts and nuts and screws and fasteners and washers. His sister and her husband owned a grocery store in Swanzey. They worked hard and did well, and every time we went to their house we could have all the soda and ice cream we could eat. We'd ride home with our bellies hard and full. Sometimes he'd stop at her house on his way home from work and she'd load him down with all good stuff. My father would bring these little tastes into the house, like coconut and pineapple and Sara Lee cakes and garlic salt and sardines.

I see, as I look back, that he was a good man, and not just in the sense that most men are good. It's more than that to me, but he drank an awful lot and in time the drinking killed him. I think it's the only story I tell, over and over again. It has a way of being behind every word, and all because I'm trying to get it right, all because I'm trying to say, This is me, too.

THE BUS HEAVED into Brattleboro, Vermont, and I got off and hitchhiked across the Connecticut River into Keene. It was no sweat getting a ride, because I was in my own part of the world again and somebody recognized me. It was someone I was related to, or someone I played ball with or against, or drank with, or dealt with, or fought with, or hung out with for a while, or hated, or loved, or smoked pot with, or worked with, and this could as easily describe one person as it could describe a whole raft of people I knew. I told them where I was going and they said they were sorry or said, yeah, they'd heard about my father and they were sorry, or there weren't any questions and they drove me right up to the doors of the hospital. As much as I hated hospitals, I walked in and got directions to where he was and went up there and found him in the sad, hushed hospital room. I dropped my knapsack on the floor like I'd come to stay where the source of light was so apparently electric.

His face was white and misshapen and bruised purple and black and yellow on one side from where he hit the corner of a desk when the seizure took him down to the floor. He was constantly working his lips to get them a little moisture and clutching at the white dressing gown. His hands trembled and shook and his knees wobbled, and he'd look at them as if they were someone else's hands and knees and it was all a mystery to him why they were behaving the way they were. The word *frail* came into my head and has stayed there ever since, his condition displacing him too often in my mind.

He bummed a cigarette and I lit it for him and then he seemed to forget about it. When he remembered it and reached for it, it caught on his dry lips, and his dry fingers slid out to the end, to the ember, and I watched those fingers burn and waited for him to feel the burn, but pain was traveling too slowly in his sedated mind. Then he did feel it and like a lame man he tried to pull his fingers away and snap the pain from their tips into the air. He lost his balance on the edge of the bed where he was sitting, and I caught him and was amazed at how light he was, how easily I could unweigh him from the earth and hold him up in my arms.

I felt that I was too young to have to be doing such a thing, but I was the only one there and didn't have my druthers. He groaned and I set him back on the bed and he was content for a while before he went to flicking away at the front of the gown. The spiders and bugs were still getting to him, and he pointed at the radiator and told me that little fellow was back, that little green man, sitting on the radiator hood.

This is the affliction of those made crazy with their alcohol dreams—spiders and insects and the seeing of little green men—and I know it to be consistent, and yet I wonder why the brain would visit such hallucinations upon its host. Why spiders and bugs and little green men? How desperate the mind must be to save itself, to frighten the body from its deadly desires. But why does it wait so long to invoke the spiders and little men? Couldn't it be more prompt, more on the spot, and from what millennium do the little green men and spiders come from? Has the brain not kept up with the modern age? How horrifying can those images be when braced against mushroom clouds, the killing fields, the camps?

Maybe the mind is like God in that he lets us do way wrong before he calls us in. Maybe the mind respects all its parts and gives license until it invokes itself so desperately to save itself. Maybe the truth is that we fear the snake more than the bomb.

Maybe because we know God made the snake and it was only men who made the bomb.

My father asked for another smoke and wanted to know if the television was on and what was on it and was it worth watching. He mumbled, and tried to work up spit and couldn't and stared off at nothing. He dozed off, so I plucked the cigarette from his mouth and butted it out in a Dixie cup half full of warm ginger ale and looked out the window. The lights in the parking lot that night seemed more bleak and sad than any darkness could have been. Then he woke up and called for the nurse, and when she didn't come he began to growl, low and deep and hurt like a wounded animal, until finally he was howling in the white room.

The nurse came and told him how he shouldn't be so loud and how he wasn't supposed to be smoking, but I knew she was telling it to me. I said I was sorry about the smoking, it was my fault, but she didn't much acknowledge my presence except for a nod of her head. She acted like I wasn't there, as if she knew how to honor my presence and respect my aloneness at the same time. To my thinking, it was what made her a good nurse.

Then she told the air that visiting hours were up, so I knew I'd have to be leaving soon. After she left, I said my good-bye.

My father said good-bye, too, and called me by my brother's name and I realized he thought I was my brother. I remember being hurt for a long time afterwards that he didn't recognize me. It gave me cause to wonder myself who I was and to think how my brother bore my father's name and how he was maybe saying good-bye to himself also.

After his stay in the hospital, his health insurance helped pay for him to go to a dry-out facility that winter, a kind of country club for alcoholics. He was there with some very famous drunks, some of whom are still alive. They are people you'd know and admire—actors and politicians and personalities and relatives of actors and politicians and personalities. He seemed to think it was all quite funny, but that was his way. He was witty and judgmental, liked being alone, but was often given over to self-pity, as are most people.

After his stay there he came home. He'd put on some weight and taken to ginger ale, chocolate bars, M&M's, and peanut brittle, and he told stories about his famous new afflicted acquaintances. But it was too late, because some time ago he'd already increased his tolerance for alcohol, already had the need to drink first thing in the morning, and wouldn't talk about it.

Already he knew how remorse worked and had given up all other interests. He avoided people and there were problems at work; there was trouble on the highway; there were irrational resentments, and that's when I found out it hadn't been his first seizure, there'd been blackouts before.

He didn't like food much anymore and couldn't much hold it down. Maybe he'd eat a grilled cheese sandwich, or an English muffin daubed high with peanut butter so thick it would cake on his gums and he'd choke and have to finger them clean. Even now I can't drink or eat those things—ginger ale, English muffins, peanut butter— without remembering my father having them.

What was left to come were the tremors and night sweats, the sneaking of liquor because it was banned in the house, the cycle of drinking and drying out, drinking and drying out, and all the while a decreasing tolerance for liquor, physical deterioration, and injuries as his days conformed to the drinking.

The doctor told my mother that what my father went through with that seizure would have killed a younger man, and years later my mother confessed to me, tears in her eyes, that she sometimes wished he'd had the dispensation of a quick and merciful death like that handed down to young drunks, one that left no other victims. She judged herself harshly for feeling that way, for giving in to her human side, and I have done the same. This is not the story I would have my father known by. It is not fair to him, but here I have gone and told it.

My father drank, I think, because it made him feel warm and cozy, made him feel love shining through from the inside out, made him feel his emotions soothed. I think it's the story I've been given to tell in this life, especially now that I'm a father and soon to be older than he ever was.

My father disappeared in February 1984. He was found dead in the forest, curled up at the foot of a tree not far from the house, and when I got the news I was in New York State. I was in the forest, too, running a chain saw, cutting cordwood for the next year's fires. I shut down the saw and sat in the cold snow against a tree, just like him, without even knowing it was the how and the where of his death. I felt pain, and tiredness and relief, and then pain again, and I sat there for a long time. Then I got up and went home to bury my father.

Fire

THAT SUMMER OF 1972, when I was eighteen, I could feel in my bones, in my flesh, the inexorable turning of my life. In a few weeks I was leaving a place where people never thought about leaving. For two centuries my mother's family was born here and lived here and was buried here under the ground a stone's throw from where they sank their plows. Not only was I leaving, but I was leaving for good. Did I know that then? No. But to even have such a thought was to be born different.

That summer when I was eighteen and most aware of what courage I lacked, most aware of how ill-suited I was for the world outside myself, the world away from the farm, the old man was to have his aerial photograph for reasons of his own, and I was the one given responsibility for the endeavor.

At the end of that day, in the gold-shot dusk, we finished up, the new-cut brush piled on top of brush that'd been laid up since winter, laid up with the butt ends to the wind. It doesn't make the most sense to burn brush in summer, but it isn't a common, everyday thing to have an aerial photograph taken, isn't common to have your grandfather who isn't talking to you take you into his confidence regarding the imminence of his death.

We'd pitched on the sumac and berry bushes and the downed limbs we'd bucked up, the willows we'd mowed from over the leech field and the slab of beech from off the tree that had been shuddered through by lightning a week before. Mixed in was the other refuse we'd rounded up and trucked down the back road.

I told Tucker and Billy they could take off and I'd light this up a little later, maybe meet them in Brattleboro after dark to drink up as much of that town as we could. Told them we'd have a really big time.

The old man came back about then and we were alone, so he could talk to me. He told me that if I stayed on the farm and worked for a hundred and twenty-five dollars a week and banked a hundred of it I'd be a rich man off in some not-so-distant future, the precise date of which he had yet to calculate. What do you say to someone who thinks like that on your behalf? I shrugged and smirked and spat in the dust, and he kept up his talk about the future, the coming depression, this old fool and that old fool. Finally, I asked him if there was something of me he wanted in particular, as was usually the case.

"Yes," he said. "Did you find a box with a brand-new horse blanket?"

"No."

"Did you look?"

"No," I said, and then I told him someone ought to tend the fire once it was lit, and I supposed it would be me.

"Fire's all right," he said. "It can take care of itself, but do what you want."

"What do you need with a horse blanket anyways?

"I don't imagine it's any of your business, but I was going to swap it."

"Swap it for what?"

"Now, you're so smart, you tell me. What would you swap a horse blanket for?"

I told him I didn't know, said it more like I didn't much care either, which sent him off on a rampage about life for me after his death. That seemed to make him feel better, and after he left, I did, too.

In the village, I called Afton from the pay phone, told her I was on my way. I made the drive to the lake and waited across the road in the pickup truck. Afton came out the door and I could see her in the porch light. She studied the light, and I wondered whether she was thinking about the light or something else. I decided to try patience and waited, and then I decided against patience and flashed the lights, telling her I was there and waiting for her to cross over to me.

I want to say she didn't walk so much as she floated, didn't move so much as she came to be in different places. She covered ground in a distracted sort of way, walked erect, walked from her hips and thighs the way a dancer does, walked as if she enjoyed the taking in of everything, as if she was thinking: I am walking now, and isn't that interesting, and if I keep going I will soon be someplace else.

As she got near to me, I shifted to neutral and held the brake. I reached over to open the passenger door, and in the dome light I could see her silver rings and more silver dangling from her ears, could see she was soaking wet, her cotton dress clinging to her body in creases and folds and shadows. I could see her body held inside her dress.

She settled in and pulled the door shut as I let off the brake, and the truck began to roll slowly, picking up speed as it coasted down the road. I clutched and shifted and let out the clutch, and the truck lurched and the engine jumped to life, the headlights blazed and trimmed over the blacktop, light for the high-ply tires growling away beneath us.

My voice was caught in my throat and in my chest. I did not know what to say, could not speak. I felt that me and Afton were on a great adventure, felt like we had to flee from the lives of all the other people who on that night did not exist on the face of the earth.

"In the summer, I like to get dressed right after I take my bath," she said. "I never use a towel. I like to feel being wet inside my clothes."

I had no idea whom she was talking to. I wanted to ask her if she felt the way I did about the world's being empty and our fleeing its emptiness, but I didn't, because I'd have died if I'd found out she didn't feel the exact same way I did. But I did know the far-off look in her eyes when she spoke like that. It was a look that frightened me.

So I'd say, What do you see and what are you thinking and earth to Afton, earth to Afton, and she'd turn her eyes on me and I would feel myself begin to grow stronger.

"If you want to look," she said, the lilt of a smile in her voice, "you should look now, because when I dry I disappear and you can't see me anymore."

I turned to take my looks, brief and lingering. The dashboard was green and the cab lights were yellow and the moon was white and all that light was on her, her body contoured with shadow and color, and then the tires snored in the loose sand on the shoulder and brush swacked against her door and I pulled us back on the road, which she must have thought was pretty funny because she laughed.

"Am I okay?" she asked, and this time I could tell she meant it, she really wanted to know if she was okay in my eyes.

You are very okay, I said, and it was by far not the most stupid thing I'd ever said to a girl, not even close. I reached under the seat, where I had a six-pack of Utica Club, and she opened up beers and we drank as we drove the dry gravel roads. She kept saying, Faster, faster, and I obliged her, taking the truck up to fifty, sashaying the bends, the tires like the rake of waves at the edge of the ocean, kicking stones against the wheel wells and sounding out in the night, and the speed making the black wind roar through the turned-out fly windows and the air like torrents of water drying her cotton summer dress.

On left-hand turns she'd be held fast to her door, and on the sharp right turns she came tipping over to my side, giggling and spilling beer into the air.

"Okay," she said. "Now we should stop doing that so we don't get hurt."

So I slowed down and we lolled along the tangle of back roads under a bower of heavy trees, and behind the heavy trees, the dark black glowing of the pines. The air had a cool tang to it, was dampening, and there were mists rising in the ditches, mists in the bottomless swamps and the wetlands, with their tannic water and skunk cabbage and fleshy greenery and buttressed trees with exposed roots and blackened leaves.

We passed by sidehill farms and mowings and corn-fields and caught the silhouetted hulks of Holsteins grazing the fence lines that ran down to the road, caught them in the light, stooping onto their knees to snag tufts of grass under the bottom strand of barbwire.

These cows belonged to a farmer who some years from now, on another August night, will be burned out. I will have come back home for a visit and Afton will be with me and we'll be parked in my mother's driveway, asleep in a Dodge van. My mother will yell out to me and I'll look off to a horizon painted red and aglow, brilliant with the distant radiance of apparent heat. Afton will go into the house and I will go to the farmer, who will be running around barefoot and shirtless, trying to save his cows from the fire. My uncle will be here, too, and my brother and my boy cousins. The town will turn out and fire departments from surrounding towns will arrive on the scene and we'll lay down a mile of hose to the river to pump and relay and pump again its silty water. The fire will burn all night and everything will be lost except the cows.

The fanner will sell and move to New York State, where land is cheap, and two years before the time of this telling, my mother will call me on the phone with the news that Ralph's wife went off to church and returned to find him dead in the silo, caught up by the unloader and crushed by its awful power.

She'll say, Ralph, he was one of the good guys.

The old man won't go to the fire, just like he wouldn't go to Cy's the morning Cy stroked, but he did ride up to Ralph's the next day and offer to buy his cows.

"What do you wish for?" Afton said to me.

She said it two or three times, but I was some kind of deaf and some kind of mute and could not make the words come to my mouth. I couldn't say I wanted to get between her legs, get my whole body between her legs and have her swallow me up; couldn't say I wanted to know her and have her know me and have us love each other forever. Couldn't say I wanted to marry her.

I slowed down to a safe speed and drove one-handed and held the shift with the other hand as we came off the mountain roads and along the River Road. Our corn was planted up to the edge there and looked like tall men, tall women, holding hands in the sweep of headlights. Afton kicked off her sandals and crossed her legs on the seat. The hem of her dress rose up and she went, Whoops, and caught it in her hands and tucked it down between her legs. I was carrying that high-chest feeling of a brick lodged where my neck flowed out into my shoulders. I decided to tell her what I wished for but instead I said, "I don't know. I wish I was a man."

She told me I was, and it wasn't just a polite thing to say. She took my hand from off the gear shift and held it on her knee. Her skin was smooth, and she stretched out that leg to put her foot in my lap. I held her foot and knew she was watching me to see what I'd do next, and I stroked the calf of her leg and held my hand like love on the flesh behind and below her knee and then up her leg to the inside of her thigh, and I waited to feel some thin fabric. It wasn't there, only heat and wetness and the slick folds of her body.

I watched the gravel road and made my slow turns, the transmission thumping, in need of downshifting, and I reached over with my left hand so not to have to take my right hand from where it was, not ever. I stole a glance and her look was fully on me and she was smiling, and so I smiled until I thought my face must have to be breaking.

She took my hand and began kissing it, licking my palm, and when she was sucking on my fingers was when I missed the next turn and drove thirty yards into a storm of field corn, the cobs battering the front end of the truck and both mirrors shearing off before I could come to a halt. Afton's legs closed on my hand and she sighed and let her head back on the seat.

I remembered cold Oswego and how like wires we were, alive and sparking to the touch, how we needed to pull away to stay alive beside that lake. Here was the melting, the fusing, and the reason to be. She clutched at my T-shirt, got a hold of my ear, and pulled me to her until our mouths were hard against each other and our teeth clicked and our noses rubbed, and she held me by fistfuls of my T-shirt, by fistfuls of my hair.

"How 'bout in the back?" she said like, Wouldn't that be fun? I thought about the back of that truck, full of axes and barbwire, a salt lick, oil cans, bale twine, feed bags, chaff, and sawdust, and so I got on my knees on the floor, knelt on the old man's new horse blanket, could feel a pair of fence pliers under my kneecap and didn't care, and then it happened like this: she unbuckled my blue jeans and they dropped and she scooted forward and that was it.

I was inside her and she was lifting my T-shirt over my head and lifting her cotton dress and then we did not move. We could not move, as if that was enough for now, as if to move would risk the world, and God must know that feeling or he would not have made it.

I held her by the small of her back and felt the bones in her back under her skin, felt them being made over into wings and felt like the strongest man in the world.

She made breath and sounds like whimpers, and then she was coming at me, surrounding me, and I slid my hands down and felt her legs, felt through to her tendons, and moved my hand up and felt her neck and the shallows of her collarbone, fine bone by fine bone, and down to her hips and thighs and ribs, and felt the lift and spring of each rib bone and the hold of each muscle and imagined the course of her blood, and she began to tremble and say my name until I was on my haunches, my back against the dashboard and she kept coming at me and I came inside her and she said my name over and over and came all around me, and then we held each other and my blood and my breathing were like trains in my body and she was still. She shivered, so I held her more tightly, and then she was still again and there was quiet.

We stayed like that, weightless and aloft, fluent with height like the air above the ground. I wondered what we must look like from the sky, from far away. Were we small and did we glow light? I thought her name and then I thought, Everything that has ever happened will never happen again. And whatever has been will never be again, and at that moment it was as if I could see my spirit float away, small, like a hummingbird or a butterfly or a puff of smoke, and it hovered about the cab until it landed on Afton, behind her ear, by the dangle of her earring, and then it seeped into her and that's where it's been forever more.

We moved slowly, tentatively, uncoupling, untangling ourselves, taking our time, as if we'd been in an accident, as if the truck had turned over and somewhere along the way we'd been operated on.

Afton pulled her dress over her head and let it fall, put her feet on the dash, and arranged her skirt to ride up on her thighs. She cleared her throat. She held her hand on my leg and made my kneecap wobble under the skin. I could still feel the sting of the imprint of those pliers.

I slid to the driver's side and started the engine and backed out of the corn. She turned so as to ride with her bare feet out the window and her head in my lap, her hair fanned out like my thigh was the pillow in Oswego.

"I wish I could see the stars," she said after a couple miles, and I thought about how there were torches back at the farm in the machine shed and how, if I could get my leg to stop shaking, I could cut the truck's roof off in a few minutes. I had a book that showed every star and I could point to them and tell her their names.

"We have to start a fire," I said, and by the way she moved I knew she was smiling.

"Burn, baby, burn," she said, just words, sparks coming out her smiling mouth.

I kept on to the farm and she sat up a bit and opened beers for us, and it wasn't until we hit the side road to the lower meadow that my leg stopped shaking.

"I like this," she said. "Starting a fire. Everything is always so important."

I liked her saying that and told her so. It was like she was audience to me as much as I was to her and we were acting life for each other, living to perform, to impress, to be hero and heroine, to be significant in each other's eyes.

This is how it is with boys and men, and I'm not ashamed to tell it. We puff and strut. We want to be cause. We want to be the reason. We want to think we can heal and inflict and fly and hover and save and forge and destroy and build again. We really think we can do those things and we know that women can, and so we want to hold on to women, want not to be found out for even our smallest weaknesses. It's simple. Men are as good and as bad as women think they are.

"I love fire," she said as I rustled up something to kindle the small flame that by night's end would consume the entire heap me and Tucker and Billy had worked to build.

"I adore you," she said. "I'm so afraid I want to stay

with you." And I was listening and hearing every word and committing each one to memory.

"There used to be a dance hall here," I said, and then I told her about Cy because he was the one who told me about the dance hall. I told her how he drank ginger water in the heat because it slaked his thirst better than water, and how he made it with water and vinegar and ginger, and how one time he was to destroy some kittens and we emptied the kittens out of the sack and filled it with stones and he earned that sack of stones up the mountain and fired into it, splintering stone, peppering his leg. I could not shut myself up. I wanted to tell her everything I knew.

"Sometimes I can hear the music and I can see them dancing," I said, and that was all it took. We were dancing by the gaining fire, her cheek on my chest and her hands up and holding me by the back of my neck, and my hands on her hips and ass and at the small of her back like when we were making love.

We danced close and were surrounded by shimmering motes that sluiced the air as the fire made gas and liquid and welded and melted and fused and glazed. The sky was made starless by murmuring, then crackling, evanescent light, made silent by the keening flames that sawed in their own wind as they flashed high, vanishing and transitory. We were swathed in that fleeting light, and all the while the source of that light was marking the earth and altering the air.

"When I was a little girl," Afton said, "one time we lived near a golf course that was next to a cemetery and I wandered away from the house and onto the golf course. My parents didn't know where I was and were really worried. They thought I was lost in the cemetery. Maybe I'd fallen into a grave. When they found me, my father told me about the golf monster. It wore plaid knickers and spit golf balls. It had six arms with a club in each hand, and fire shot from the top of its head and it ate little girls. I told that story to my psychology professor and she thought it was a harsh punishment. She thought I should seek help, but I told her no, everything was okay. I never got lost again."

"Tucker won't set foot in a cemetery. He says he'll spend enough time there as it is."

"Yeah, and I say, so what? It works for him. Why is it everyone needs everyone else so much?"

"This is now a fire," I said, and gave myself over to admiring it and wanted her to do the same, to give her cares over to its combustion. It was the burning of wood and brush, festooned with medicine bottles and lubricants, salves and filters, boxes and powders, tubes and syringes, fuels and additives, cleansers and soaps and ammonia, abrasives, gaskets and liners, plastic piping and rubber hoses.

It burned hesitantly and then with fury and passion. It popped and geysered and groaned and hissed and exploded. It showed vermilion and carmine. It took the temper from metals, made gas of aluminum, set glass to bubble. It showed cerise, spasmed out purplish and reddish light. Cans exploded, and caps and lids popped and spiraled and spun. Glass melted, and ash and drift wove helical patterns in the night sky, wove sky-high into the ether.

I could see the light burning off the studded brush piles flash in her cheekbones and her hair, and behind us were our shadows, thrown high and wide and glowering as they wrapped from the earth to the trees to come round above us, and we were over our heads.

And then, as the fire became only a steady rumble, I heard an engine start and headlights shot forth from the bluff over our heads and backed away, the beams whisking in the sky as the tires bumped on the uneven ground.

He'd come to see his fire and now he had seen it and in the morning there'd be something else, a new adventure, a feat he wanted to commit someone to so he could see it unfold and be reminded of what it was to be young and immortal. Maybe Cy was with him, maybe someone else. No matter, he was now always alone, whomever he was with, his body dying but his mind still hard and sly and sharp and capable.

"Who's that?" Afton said.

"I think it was him," I said. "I think he wanted to see his fire. He wanted to see if a bonfire was how he remembered it. I think that's all."

I realized then that I would always want to have someone between me and life, that I would always be afraid of people. I remembered how she told me in Oswego, Heal yourself, heal yourself, and how I wanted to say, I have unstitched myself because of you. Don't tell me that. Don't tell me to heal myself. The old man was dying and my own father had begun his descent and in a few weeks I'd be gone from here. I wanted fire, too. I wanted what God promised to come next after he flooded the earth.

"Sometimes I worry we're too far gone," she said, and I didn't know if she meant we were far gone good or far gone bad, and I wanted to ask such a dumb question.

"I wish we could always be together," I finally said, trusting her with my truest wish, and she looked at me as if to say, Not yes and not no.

At the fire's smolder, the gray of morning began to show. The upper arch of the sun's disk was coming above the ocean's horizon some hours away, and as much as I never wanted to sleep again in my life, my tiredness hit me like a hammer. Afton held my head and said for me to close my eyes for a moment as we lay under the night wrapped in the horse blanket. She said she would hold me, and when I woke up I realized we'd been out all night and that was maybe not a good thing.

I touched her face and she stirred in my arms, waking up to say, "Wait. I thought we all died."

"You were having a dream," I said, and told her we should get out of there and placed my hand on her blanketed hip and gently squeezed. But we did not move. We waited for the sunrise and together, under that horse blanket, we felt the cold that precedes the dawn. I didn't know how we'd explain and I didn't care.

We'd say we fell asleep, say we got a flat tire. We'd lie or tell the truth, or something like the truth. We stayed out all night to tend the fire and it was a good thing, too, because it went wild, threatened to burn a hole straight through to China. It would have scorched their asses. Would have left them nothing but char, and we are now holy to all the missionaries, to all the people who loved

The Good Earth, and those Chinese people are now ready to be baptized and Mao himself, with his Communist ass, is first in line.

We made love again on the horse blanket in the earliest morning. Afton wanted us to pray after we made love the second time, wanted us to pray to some vague God who seemed doting and benign by the way she talked to him. She wished his judgment would not be severe and told him she'd be disappointed if it was. She told him we were doing the best we could with what he gave us, said she was speaking for me, too, amen.

Then she whispered, "You know, sometimes when I am almost asleep, I can hear my blood, and sometimes I can hear my eyes blink."

The White Barn

I SMELLED LIKE the burning that early morning and would be sweating it out all day long. Sometimes what you're doing gets inside you, inside your guts, and you begin to smell like the job, your breath and your sweat. They come out like ensilage or hay or grain or cows, or if you've been fishing or cleaning fish, they come out like the river or trout, or if you've been hunting or cleaning game or slaughtering animals, the smells come out like pheasant or ducks or deer or hogs or beef or even sweetly sour, like milk, or sweet and fumy, like gas or diesel.

That morning I smelled like the burning and I smelled like Afton, her perfumed skin, her body, and like what we'd done in the dark and the first light, and the smells came together in my head to mean all the same. So when I pulled in from taking her back to her grandmother's cottage and saw the fire trucks parked n the drive, I thought something had rekindled and come up the land. Feeling guilty about that and so many other things, I thought, I'm sorry, I'm sorry. I didn't mean to do it.

But it wasn't that at all. They'd come to dress up the place like Tucker had suggested, to wash it down like tomorrow was Sunday and the whole farm was going to church. The old man was sitting on the porch in his stocking feet and undershirt, his suspenders draping to the floor. He was tapping his cane and chewing tobacco, calmly anticipating the onset of his latest production. Later on, my mother would speculate that he got the cancer from swallowing tobacco juice and its coming out the other end. I think that is either a really smart idea or an utter impossibility.

I could see him motioning for me to come over but acted like I didn't and started for the barn. I didn't get very far before he bellowed out my name like a summons. I could hear his voice over the pumper priming and flushing to build a head of water, and so I had to turn and go back.

He looked at me and smiled, not what you'd call a friendly smile, more like the cat to the mouse. But it had its appeal. I stood off the porch and we watched as the volunteer firemen got out their hoses and began blasting water on the buildings, wetting them down and knocking off whatever loose paint there was, sending it to fleck the sky and, when that was done, taking after the drive, sending up waves of dirt and chaff and sawdust, blasting it clean and shiny and black as they chased everything into the ditches.

The new drive was his pride and joy. In April he had it put in, and for the first few weeks he wouldn't let anybody park on it. We had to keep the machinery off in the farthest places before he relented and said we could park on the drive, but we had to sweep it constantly. After a time it wasn't new and he was off on other delights, tormenting this person, beating that one on a deal evening up a score from twenty years back, buying and selling, and the drive began going the way of everything else. It took so much work to do the chores there was little time left for things like maintenance and upkeep. The drive took on piles of sawdust, spills of grain, oil stains, cow shit, and grease spots until it was like a piece of the farm, a piece of the earth.

Then he said to me, "What do you want?"

"What?" I said.

"What do you want?"

"You called me. I didn't call you."

He acted as if that were news to him, as if he didn't know all about me pulling in and getting out of the truck and ignoring him and walking to the barn and him calling out my name. I thought about Afton walking down the path to her grandmother's house by the lake. Would her grandmother be up and wandering the house, fretting? Would she be trying to remember something? Would she be dead, and if she was, would it be by her own hand?

But it was how Afton thought about me that was my main concern. Did she have regrets? Could she sleep? Was she asleep by now?

"Good God," he said, and stood up fast so that his trousers slipped down to his knees. He hiked them up and buttoned them, looped a suspender over one shoulder, but not before reaching inside to jostle himself. He got near me and tried to raise himself up, tried to hover over me, but he hadn't tried that in some while and he found out I was as tall and as big in the shoulders as he was and backed down.

"Good God," he said again.

The hoses were pummeling the buildings. Loose paint was skying into the air and twirling to the ground.

"You know," I said, "that old paint is probably lead-based and shouldn't be left lying around. Cows get into it, it'll poison the milk."

Another hose had started on the far corner of the drive, its water kicking up geysers of sawdust, ushering before it the wet slop it was making, and leaving the new drive glistening.

"Good God," he said.

"Good God what, for Chrissake?"

"Last night," he said, and he grinned and shook his head. "You think I can't tell?"

His face looked like a dried apple. He cracked into a full smile, something like you'd see on a carved pumpkin.

I try to see his face now, but it's the chemo face I see, hairless and almost transparent. The blue veins can be seen and tracked, and a vessel in one eye has exploded and there's a burst of blood and sometimes it looks like a wound or a sunrise or the hollow spur of columbine. I was born with a version of his face and his body come down through my mother, so to see him was to see where I'd be, to see where I'll go.

"Last night," he said. "You got your ashes hauled."

"I don't imagine that's any business of yours." *Getting your ashes hauled* was a term I was not familiar with, but there wasn't any mistaking what he was talking about.

"No, I guess it isn't," he said, and sighed as if I'd spoken an irrefutable truth, and he looked off at his firemen for a time and then came back quickly, asking, "Where's your crew? Supposed to be here."

"They'll be here," I said, and then, so as to give him something else to think about, I said, "You know it won't come out black."

"What?" he said.

I told him how the drive, how streets and roads, tar and asphalt don't come out black in photographs. They always come gray and white, and this disturbed him. He denied it to be so, told me it was black, anybody could see that, so why wouldn't it come out black like it was? He told me I was just trying to make trouble.

"Maybe it isn't really black," I said.

"Well, maybe the Christ it isn't."

I had him cornered on this one. It was a rare occasion and I was determined to enjoy it because I knew he'd get over being vexed and then he'd get cross and get even.

"Get your breakfast," he said.

I had chores to do, but he told me to get breakfast. When the old man told you to do this or that, it became a mission. So that was fine by me, and I went in and sat down to eat. Already on the table was cereal and juice and melon and coffee to pour, and my grandmother came out of the kitchen with a platter of French toast with butter and maple syrup and Canadian bacon, and I kept eating it until we were out of bread.

My grandmother laughed and wanted to know if I had a hollow leg. She got on the phone to my mother and told her to bring down some bread from her house, and my mother showed up with more bread. The first thing she wanted to know was if I had a hollow leg, but said it like she was mad, and all the while they kept bringing me more and more French toast. The women, they loved to watch the men eat, at least I think they did. I think it was more that than that they had to feed us and didn't have any way around it.

These were the women in the family. They said all wondrous things about our appetites as they brought on more plates of steaming food, food that was baked and boiled and fried, their words aghast, but their eyes gone to twinkle. They went along with most everything until they put their foot down, and then it was war if you didn't pay heed. They said when things began and ended but left the middle up to the men. They'd say, Give you an inch and you take a mile.

To the women, a big man was a *lummox* and noise was a *commotion*. They talked about mattresses, about keeping them turned and aired out. They hung their rugs up and beat them. They had remedies for prickly heat and poison ivy and all manner of itch and prescribed air for every ailment. Let the air get to it, they said. When my grandmother dressed up, she wore her good pearls and it didn't matter that they were her only pearls. When the women were all dressed up, they wore gloves and from way off you could hear the rustle of material when they walked. They ate pimento sandwiches and cucumber sandwiches, and honeycomb tripe, and there was always a sheet cake, or pie, or chocolate-chip cookies, or brownies fresh-baked at someone's house; you had to ask for the first one, but after that you could about empty the plate. They cooked pork until it was like leather. My mother could enjoy a meal of crackers and milk, poor people's food from when she was a girl. My grandmother grew peonies and irises and violets and each year tried out something new for the front lawn—a birdbath in the shape of a giant sunflower, or a windmill, or a trellis, or a barrel for growing strawberries—and when we were children, on the morning of the first of May, she'd collect us up and take us into the woods to gather flowers and greenery and berries and we'd make May baskets to leave on people's front steps. She'd tell us to knock and when we heard someone coming we were to run like the dickens back to the car.

And there were times, too, when the women would be in a room and they'd be talking and laughing and you would walk into that room and it would go all silent. They'd want to know what you wanted and you'd say you didn't want anything and they'd tell you about some sweet they'd made and hid up from everyone else, make small talk until you left to find it. It was easy to think how much they didn't need you, how easily a handful of cookies could send you off.

My mother came in with another plate of French toast. She wanted to know where I was last night. I told her I was tending the fire and I fell asleep. I told her that her father knew where I was.

"You were with her," she said.

"No, I wasn't. Just for a little while and then I took her home."

"You two were out the whole night."

"How do you know?"

"You know what you did."

My mother wasn't happy about last night, but being happy was not as high on her list as duty and obligation, service and steadfastness. I could not hang my head, though, because standing up for yourself was also more important than happiness. Once you did something, you didn't turn back on the doing. That would be a weakness. So I held my head up and did my best to look her in the eye.

"I know what I did," I said, "and that's between me and God. He'll deal with me as he will."

"Let's just say I know, too, and another thing—you better be careful, mister."

She stared into me and it wasn't hard to tell the conviction behind her words. I expected to get a talking to and I braced myself, but it didn't come and I thought she might even begin to cry. We were becoming something different for each other and she felt it long before I did. She knew I was going away in a few weeks. I'd be the first in the family to do such a thing.

She held me with her look and then turned and left me alone, and I wanted to wonder for at least a moment about what I'd glimpsed, but the old man came hustling in to take up the house with himself. He took a coffee cup to the sink and let hot water run in it. He was a big believer in preheating his coffee cup. He filled it from the percolator that was always going and sat down at the table.

"You wash up?" he hissed so no one could hear him talk to me.

I nodded and wiped syrup from my lips with the sleeve of my T-shirt.

"You did not."

He was disgusted that I'd not stood at the sink and sluiced water over my head and arms and face the way he did. He surely had his habits—like he couldn't stand the hiccups and couldn't understand how someone might lack the self-control to end them, and no one could eat potato chips in his presence, because he didn't like the sound. To this day my mother will let a potato chip soften in her mouth before she'll bite into it.

"You like that bacon," he said.

It was bacon he'd smuggled out of Canada under the seats of his New Yorker automobile. Every time he went up there to buy cows, he came back with butter and bacon under the seats, and when they'd ask him at the border if he had anything to declare, he'd say, no, he didn't.

One time we were in Quebec, in Sherbrooke, buying cows. We stayed in a motel, and when I thought he was asleep over in his bed I put a quarter in the steel box that said Magic Fingers. My bed began to hum and vibrate, and I couldn't help myself and began to laugh. The hum and the vibration came to be a terrible racket of a noise and went on for some time, and the old man was none too thrilled. He tossed and turned and cussed me out to the point where I suggested he rip the toilet out of the floor just to make himself feel better.

Don't think I couldn't if I wanted to, he said, just to set me straight.

The racket and our row kept him awake, and the next day marked the first of the times he wouldn't talk to me, no way, no how. He was going to hold me responsible for every sleepless night he'd ever had, so I decided to give him a little taste of his own medicine and not talk to him. I'd wait him out and see who gave in first.

Pulling out of Sherbrooke that morning we had some weather, one of those every-twenty-year blizzards. It was winter at its best and most cold, and we were making slow progress through the burden of snow and the buff of wind. On the highway, the snowplows were using a high-speed plowing technique, but with the towering flawy wind the snow just billowed out the top of the wing plow and filled in the void left behind. That seemed to cheer him up, seeing that something new didn't work.

The windshield wipers beat hard, and at times the old man had to power down his window, grab the near wiper, and let it smack back to free it of ice. The headlights made their way as best they could, settling out before us and sifting the snow as if the white light were a sieve and the snow were sugar. After a time I got sleepy. The sounds of the wipers and the heater fan receded and all was silent. I moved into sleep because I felt no fear with him at the wheel, had no thought that we weren't safe on the treacherous road, but then he'd say something out loud to himself. He'd curse the weather or ask God to damn this or that, and I'd come awake again. I learned that his not talking to me did not rule out my having to listen to him.

We passed through customs and into Vermont. We were to stop in Lancaster that day, on our way down the river, to see a man about a herd of cows, so we pulled into town and got sandwiches at a little grocery. They were the kind that are frozen and you microwave right there.

Microwave was something new for the times, something he wanted to try out. He said that he should get one of those for the barn, and I thought that would be a good idea, frozen steak sandwiches and hot dogs and hamburgers and meatball sandwiches and roast beef sandwiches heated up in a minute or two. He bought newspapers at the little grocery, but not to read. I never saw him read, though I knew he could. He bought them to line the car floor so we wouldn't get the mats and carpet dirty with our boots.

We took our sandwiches and sodas and newspapers and sat in the New Yorker with the motor running. The old man went to complaining to himself about how the meat stuck to the bread in his microwave sandwich and how that just wouldn't do, and when the cattle dealer showed, I got sent in for coffee.

The old man said to the cattle dealer, "I want cream, no sugar. Tell him what you'd like. He'll get it."

The cattle dealer shrugged and told me what he wanted. Nothing seemed strange to him. He knew the old man. If it wasn't one thing, it was another.

I fetched their coffee and got in the backseat so they could talk business and smoke and sip at their cups. The old man smoked Dexter cigars and the cattle dealer smoked Chesterfields and he kept dropping his ashes on the floor. There must have been an ember in one of those ashes because I began to smell smoke. They didn't notice it, because they were smoking, too.

The old man asked the cattle dealer if he had ever had a microwave sandwich and, if he had, what he thought of it.

The cattle dealer shrugged at this, too, and said he had no opinion either way, and the old man asked him if he'd ever noticed how the meat stuck to the bread. Again the cattle dealer shrugged, and the old man made a sound of disgust as if he could not imagine someone living life in such an uninspected way.

Then I could see smoke coming from under the seat, but I had made a pact with myself not to speak to the old man, so I told the cattle dealer instead, told him he was on fire. At that moment there was a sudden lick of flame, and after that it was assholes and elbows as we fled the New Yorker and began pouring in handfuls of new snow.

That little occurrence in Lancaster ended business with the cattle dealer. The old man had no patience for being set afire. He'd go on to use it against him as a reason for not doing business until the guy was ready to cut his throat to make a deal.

After the great car fire of Lancaster, we headed south toward home, fighting the weather all the way, with the windows cracked open for the cold stench of smoke and burned carpet. I was a little disappointed when I realized

I probably hadn't missed any school by going to Quebec with the old man.

Forty miles north of the farm came a clearing under the sky, under the night's unweighing, and for the rest of our passage the snow in the hills was like some confection, the high white meadows like scars of marble, the pine trees palming the snow in momentary perfection. The clearing stayed until we reached the farm, and then the blizzard closed in behind us like a disappearing wake and it snowed for the rest of the week, leaving no trace of another world beyond the farm.

I spent those days outside, plowing snow to keep lanes open for equipment, for the grain truck and the milk truck. The morning of the first day, I got into the old man's car to move it so I could get through with the loader. Inside the car, in the cold air, I could still smell the smoke and then the smell of salty butter coming from behind the seat. Looking back there, I found a frozen yellow pool, speckled with soot.

The story of the great car fire of Lancaster got told like it was my fault: He saw the flames but kept his mouth shut. He was the one smoking. He was playing with matches in the backseat. He did it on purpose. He's a pyromaniac.

But most people only believed what he said because it was him saying it. They believed his pronouncements the way a minister is believed in his own church, a doctor in a hospital, a child come from dream sleep. That butter had melted and taken on ash and smoke, and it wasn't until he sold the car in the spring that the smell went away.

"No more fires," he whispered, my grandmother and mother still in the kitchen. "You left a big black spot down there that will show up in the picture. Probably ruin it. Damn thing probably isn't even worth taking now, and make sure all those paint chips get picked up. That paint's got lead in it, and those cows get into it, it'll poison the milk."

I nodded and sponged at the maple syrup and melted butter on my plate.

"And another thing," he said, nodding toward the kitchen. "Don't get them excited. It's bad enough we have to live with them."

I wanted to tell him it was his idea to burn all that junk and rubbish, not mine. I wanted to tell him it was almost a mile from the farm and ask how high up did he think this picture would come from anyway. Wanted to tell him I already figured on having to rake and rake the ditches to get up the paint chips. But I didn't.

I kept on eating my French toast and Canadian bacon, and then I ate a muffin with blackberry preserves and had another glass of milk and took my dishes to the kitchen, thanking my mother and grandmother for breakfast, and left the house.

Outside, the volunteer firemen were packing up. Tucker and Billy had arrived and were sitting in the open side door of the van. The old man came out there, too, admiring the inside of the van like he wanted one for himself just like theirs. He headed off to the fire trucks and the volunteers, where he'd have a hundred questions to pester them with, questions he already knew the answers to.

"Got to go to Keene and pick up some stuff," Tucker said. "Today we're painters."

"All of us?"

"He didn't say otherwise."

So we piled into Tucker's van, and when we got to Keene, Tucker wanted to stop by his brother's apartment. He didn't say why; he just wanted to stop. We went up the stairs and at the top of the landing the apartment door was wide open and the smell of vomit and beer and pot was like a wall you had to pass through to gain entrance.

Tucker's brother was passed out on the sofa, one hand on the floor, palm up, and his other hand holding his crotch. The apartment looked like it'd taken a direct hit from something that started out in space and had plenty of time to build up speed. Tucker's brother was a fullback, a senior when I was a sophomore, and one day I took him head-on and felt it down through my body, felt that my body was a tuning fork and he had just dropped me off the piano.

Now his body was thick and ponderous and his hair was long and his beard hung to his chest. He had a low number in the draft and was facing a physical, so he had been gorging on food and beer and cold medicine to raise his blood pressure to a level too dangerous for the service. Right now he was supposed to be at work. He was a carpenter and word was he hadn't showed in a week. His tools were strewn about the single room and there was a fan in the window, nicking backwards on an incoming breeze.

"Get up," Tucker said, pushing at his brother's shoulder, but his brother only groaned, flicking at the air with his fingers. "Get up, you lazy son of a bitch."

"Hey, let it rest," I said.

"No one's heard from him in days," Billy said. "His mother's been trying to get ahold of him, but he won't answer the phone. Tucker says she's worried sick."

By now Tucker was slapping his brother's face, saying, "Get up. Get to work," "Call home," "Clean yourself up," "Take a fucking bath," but his brother would only swallow and lick his lips and make noises and swat at the air and go back to how he was.

"Let's go," Billy said. "You can tell her you stopped and tell her he's okay."

But Tucker wouldn't leave off. He paced about and kicked at the boots and clothes strewn across the floor. He found a dime bag, pocketed it, then shook his brother again. He couldn't get a rise out of him, so that's when Tucker plugged in the circular saw and, in an eye blink, zipped off his brother's beard so close I could see the pink of his brother's chin. Tucker held the beard up like a bloodless scalp, unplugged the saw and set it on the floor, and placed his brother's hand on the handle. He stuffed the beard in the other hand, the one his brother held his crotch with, and we thought that was pretty funny in an odd sort of way.

I think we were all strangers to our time, always being thrown back on ourselves. This is the way it has always been, young people being asked both to wise up and to play dumb. There and then, coming home nightly, were the pictures and the stories of the newly dead and the still alive, stories of the casualties away and at home, and all the while we were being told who and what we were and the serious consequences of our actions. It didn't stack up. We had our suspicions. There were a lot of people who said, Go to hell, and walked, and there are some who didn't and never will forget.

By the time we got to the paint store, Tucker had cooled down, but you could cell that wasn't the end of it. There'd be civil war for a time. The guy at the paint store had the loading dock stacked with five-gallon buckets of white paint, fifteen in all, and ten gallons of black, and a box of brushes that looked awful puny.

"Holy shit," Tucker said. "We'll never get to Mexico."

"Fuck this," Billy said. "That's not what I call 'a little painting, just a little touch-up here and there, boys.'"

I didn't say much one way or the other. All that paint left me defeated. It was as if it stood between me and my way to somewhere else. All that paint to be pushed before I could leave, and I thought of it in just that way. I sat down on a bucket and bummed a smoke off Tucker while he and Billy kept up their rant.

"I could rent you a sprayer," the guy said to me, "but when I offered it to your grandfather he insisted on brushes."

"A sprayer?" I said.

"Why, yes, of course. A sprayer."

We went inside, where he had a brand-new airless spray rig. It was a beauty to behold. That thing could lay on a four-foot-wide band of paint as fast as you could walk. It drove that paint with so much pressure it'd send the paint into your skin if you held your hand under the spray of it. By way of warning, the guy told us of one man who did just such a thing and his fingers had to be amputated.

"We'll go with the sprayer," I said.

Needless to say, the old man went apeshit, a genuine full-blown rage. He broke a cane and blew a few vessels in the soft skin below his eyes. It just wasn't the way he wanted it done. Finally it was Tucker who made peace, showed him how he'd save money in labor so the whole thing would come out cheaper in the end.

Okay, that was all well and good, but he was convinced the paint wouldn't stay on. He claimed that brushed-on paint was better than sprayed-on paint because brushed-on paint was paint you worked into the wood while sprayed-on paint was just a coating. Tucker told him the paint-store manager guaranteed it, and all the while I was imagining painters to be men with forearms the size of milk jugs with all that working in of the paint.

Billy became the spray man, riding in the bucket because he had no fear of heights and a center of gravity like a cat, and Tucker ran the loader because it was easy, and I stirred paint and kept the reservoir full. It was all very good work, quite simple, yet with enough procedures to make it appear learned and complicated.

Cy dragged a water hose over to where I was, for me to have a drink and so he could watch the work. He'd been hoeing in my grandmother's garden and was very tired. Day by day his face had become less wizened and more boylike, as if to make the undertaker's job not so difficult. He gestured with the hose and I took a drink. The water was cold and hard. It came from the springhouse off the mountain. He asked me if my father had any home brew and I told him he didn't. It'd been ten years since my father made home brew, but it didn't seem worth explaining.

I thought about the gloom and webs that must make thick the work of his brain, thought about Afton's grandmother losing her memory. I thought of the water Cy brought me as something he was sharing. I thanked him and he clasped an arm to his waning self and seemed to not know what he was doing. Then he took out a pipe and held it in his hand, staring at it, and I understood. I took it from him and reached into his shirt pocket for his pouch. I tamped the bowl full and lit it and handed it back to him, and he did take pleasure in that smoke. The reservoir began a sucking noise, so I had to dump in more paint, and when I looked up, Cy was wandering away.

At noon, I went in for lunch and the old man was on the phone. He was talking as quietly as he could but the volume was rising. He was saying, "Well, by Jesus, the goddamn thing is black and I want it to be black . . . You're sure you can . . . About making it come out black, I'm telling you . . . You're sure you can."

I sat down, and when he hung up the phone I asked what that was all about.

He glanced to the kitchen where my grandmother was preparing lunch and got his chin up in the air and said, "I don't imagine it's any of your business, but he said it'd be black."

Water

I DIDN'T HAVE an excuse for taking the truck that night but I took it anyway. I could have made up a story, could have pulled into the pump and filled it with gas and said I had to go to Keene for a machine part or up to the other farm to check the heifers.

I wouldn't be stealing the gas if I took it, because I would be doing it where anyone could see me. I knew the difference, because the last two winters I'd spent my nights drinking in the bars in Vermont where the drinking age was eighteen, and eighteen meant you could get served if you were sixteen and looked eighteen. So to steal gas was when you had money and wanted to save that money for beer and whiskey. To steal gas was to shut off the engine and roll the car into the pump when it was late and the house was dark, so you could make the run to the bars in Brattleboro or Bellows Falls.

Years later, after everyone died—my grandfather, my father, and then my grandmother—my mother moved back into her parents' house. One time when I was home for a stay, I slept in that front bedroom where the old man used to sleep on winter nights, and from that room I could hear everything—the bawling calves, the grunt of a cow, coy dogs on Eye Hill—and I realized the old man must have heard me every time. I hadn't gotten away with my gas stealing and I had to smile at how much he knew and never told.

Still, I needed gas, so I went up to my uncle's filling station. I liked my uncle quite a bit. He'd married into the family the same way my father had. My uncle ran his filling station before the interstate was completed, and as a consequence he got all the north–south traffic between Montreal and New York, Montreal and Boston. You run a gas station like that, you get all kinds of people passing through, some on vacation, some on the run, some up to no good, some just traveling.

My uncle was a DXer, one of those who specialize in finding distant stations on world-band radio. He had come to be one from keeping the pumps open as late as possible and needing something to occupy his mind after the networks signed off. He knew all sorts of useful and useless stuff. He played the horses and for a time ran a poker game out of a house he owned in another town.

I asked him if he wasn't worried, it being illegal and all to run a poker game, and he said he didn't know but he'd ask the chief of police that night when he saw him at the game. He always had decks of cards to give out because he ran a good game, changing decks several times a night.

I pulled up to his pumps, filled the tank, and went in to pay.

"What's the good word," he said, pleased to see me.

"I don't know."

"Legs," he said. "Spread the word."

I smiled and he laughed. I held out a five and he asked me why I was filling the truck at the station. I told him I was on personal business. He told me he'd heard all about my personal business from my aunt, who'd been told by my grandmother, who'd been told by my mother, and said my personal business seemed real fine, real beautiful. Told me the gas was on him on condition I stop back at the end of the night so we could catch up on each other's lives.

My uncle had three daughters and treated me like a son. When I was a kid, I'd pedal my bike over to his station and we'd watch the ball games on TV, and the past four years he'd come to watch me play all over the state. He was free with his advice on how I'd played and how that had bearing on all manner of life's concerns, like what kind of a man you were and what kind of a man you would be. He played ball, too, when he was a kid, and it was something he loved.

He told me he hadn't seen much of me lately and, with me going away and all, well, he wanted to talk a bit.

"Yeah," I said. "I can do that." And then he palmed me a crisp new twenty.

"Hey," he said as I was leaving, "that Tucker and Billy, you want to watch those two. I think they're up to no good. Do you think you should be hanging around with those boys?"

I told him they were leaving in a day or two, headed out west, so not to worry, and then I headed off myself.

I called Afton from the village and she said to wait there for her, she wanted to ride her bicycle to where I was. When she got there, I hoisted her bicycle over the side of the truck and we were on our way again, driving into the night, and we did not speak about the night before as we rode in mostly silence. She sat beside me on the hard seat, her legs tucked under her and her hand at the back of my neck. It was as if we were taking up where we'd left off in the early morning, only it was like the day had been a year long, or ten years long, and we were that much older and had been together that much longer. It was like we'd singed each other and could not turn away, and still, at the same time, it was like we'd left the kids with my mother or her mother and were going out to dinner or for ice cream or just for a drive. It was all that, both at rest and at the edge of collision.

There was a place we made to where the brook broke from the Granger Hollow between my house and the farm and out and into the light. It splayed there and paused and caught its breath before it began its descent to the Connecticut River, making the run through the Sheep Rocks, where I learned to swim, and over the free boulders, granite and marble, pyrites and mica sparkling in the sun. It ran on under the pine and spiky hemlock, brittle balsam and poplar, white and gray birch, and farther up the oaks and elms and maples: sugar, red, rock.

It carried the silt and flotsam and sometimes those very trees that lined the cut banks as they outweighed their tenuous grasp and a wind or a rain or a high water under them. When their scrabbly roots as thick as a man's leg could no longer hold purchase on those high, knuckly cuts, they toppled to the water and rode the brook to the river as it carved and suspended and deposited. In the spring, it carried all to the wet gray banks of clay and gravel and loam that lined the river's mazy course. Down that stretch of forest, the snow lingered until late spring, and all day long the mists rose off the back of the water as it bulled through the chutes and rode the slides. To be heard was the knocking sound of tumbling boulders, the rolling and sliding of the water's bed load.

Late in the spring the brook would settle to calf-deep, and in the summer, if it was droughty, it would come to be a trickle, would sink, would disappear for twenty or thirty feet at a stretch and then rise from the ground again, as if it had only been fooling around, playing hide and seek.

It was here I first met Afton.

I was standing on the downstream side drawing barbwire so taut it hummed in the air. I was alone, working alone, and I liked it that way.

The old man said barbwire had to float, had to give and take and still be taut. He liked to tune his barbwire, but I was young and liked it only taut and the job done. Here at the brook, it'd stay this way for ten months, until the spring runoff snapped through. It held the milk cows east of the bridge and the heifers and a bull west of the bridge while letting them water, which is all we asked until it was time to take a morning and come back and build the sixty feet of fence again.

When Afton came back the spring after we met, I was in the same place again, fixing fence. I like to think that something memorable was said, but we only smiled at each other and that was memorable enough. When I first met her I had been drawing barbwire, and when I looked up she was sitting on her ten-speed bicycle at the bridge, her elbows on the handlebars, her feet square on the ground. She was watching me and I could see her there, fronting the sun.

WE PARKED THE truck off the road that night and took the path down to the Sheep Rocks. I liked the path because it was narrow and I could follow her. Some ways down the path she stopped and said, "Could you tell me something?"

"Yeah," I said. "Anything."

"What is it about men and women's asses?"

I held out my hands, palms up, as if to say, I don't know, what do you think? She laughed at me and shook her head. I was still standing there when she turned on her heel and disappeared through the tunnel of trees. I caught up to her and grabbed her ribs and she swiped at me and we were on the run to the Sheep Rocks, where the water made a deep pool. We undressed and stepped into the dark water.

She moaned from the cold of it and then came a moonrise over the trees. The water lapped at our ankles and crickets made sounds in the woods. I felt lovesick, and

I worried that I could not rise to my imagination, that I could be without her and alone in this water.

Afton said, "Make it not so cold," and for a moment I thought I could as she slid in up to her waist and held her arms against her chest in the cold water. I slid in, too, went to her, and the cold water shrunk me away to nothing. I put my arms around her and held her. Water beads jeweled her skin and the moonlight showed off on her body.

"What did you do?" she said.

"I made it not so cold."

"How did you do that?"

"I don't know. I was just kidding."

I had a bar of Ivory soap stashed in the crevice of a rock. I wiped away the twigs and handed it to her and she began to wash my back.

"At first the man is clean," she said, "and he smells good, and then after a day or two the good smell turns sour, and if he can hold out, the sour smell turns to the earth smell. He smells like trees and the earth and that's even better, and by the seventh day he smells like creation and that makes me melt from the waist down."

At that moment she would not release me and I did not move to be released. Afterward we floated in the water, her hair loose and undulant, floating by her face and shoulders like a cloud and brushing me, sliding across my neck and chest like a wet kiss. I could hear stones turning, could see bats flicker by, and I'd let my feet touch the smooth rock on the bottom, which was like porcelain, and she let her body float straight out from mine on the current, her head back and on my shoulder. Our ears were close by, like whispery open mouths.

"Your mouth tastes different after you come," she said.

"What's it taste like?"

"Pistachio."

"What'd it taste like before?"

"I don't remember."

I knew no one who spoke as she did, knew no one whose words were like touch.

IT WAS LATE when I swung by the filling station. The pumps were shut down but there was a light on inside. When I dropped Afton off, she told me she couldn't see me for a couple days, she had some things to do and would call me, and I thought the worst, and no matter what she said my mind went all desperate. It was something I'd done to send her away, somehow she needed distance, did not need me as much as I needed her. There was no other way I could see it.

My uncle was inside. He unlocked the door and asked me if she had ditched me, said it in those words.

"Why?"

"By the look on your face."

No, I told him, nothing like that, and then he told me how women are like fish in the sea and how they are like buses. You miss one, and another will be along before you know it. I asked him what he was doing so late. He told me he was scanning the world band for a KKK station out of the South, a clandestine broadcast. I asked him where it was and he said, Well, if he knew, it wouldn't be clandestine.

"See now," he said, "this one is from Sweden. See, that's Swedish they are talking, and look here, that's English."

Then he goes, "Hey, I heard a rumor the old man had cancer. Any truth to that?"

I shrugged and said I didn't know.

"Jesus Christ," he said, "he really does."

About then a car came into the pumps and he said, "Shit," and made me get under his desk, told me not to say a word. From under there I could hear people come in and knew them to be a man and a woman by their feet. They were down from Montreal and they were friendly with my uncle, talked quietly, and laughed some. When they left, my uncle called me out. He had two piles of twenties, each as thick as a brick, on his desk. He peeled off five of them and gave them to me and told me not to spend them around there and told me I had not seen anything. I told him I had surely not seen anything and he gave me some decks of cards, too.

Then my uncle went quiet, like he was feeling what passed for sadness. I could tell his thinking, could tell he wanted to say how much he was going to miss me but couldn't really get the words together in his head.

"Hey, now remember," he said. "You've got to have a philosophy to go into life with, something to live by. Call it a life philosophy."

"Yeah," I said. "That's a good idea. Like what?"

"Like 'Blood is thicker than water' or 'Don't piss into the wind.' Like 'Don't take shit off nobody,' but that's probably someone else's. You've got to come up with your own."

"What's yours?"

"I can't tell you that," he said, and the way he said it made me think he'd chosen not such a good one for his own life.

"Well, do you know some good ones?" I said. "Maybe one that tells you more what to do than what is or tells you what not to do?"

"Oh no, there aren't any like that. Philosophies tell you what you shouldn't do so as to keep on the straight and narrow. I wouldn't trust a philosophy that did otherwise."

"Well, what should I do?"

He thought about this for me, cocked his head, and wiped at his mouth. And then he said, "Fuck the world. Do whatever you want to do and tell the world to fuck off."

We stood alone in the dimly lit station, different lives behind us and whole different lives ahead of us. There was no blood between us except what was shared by his wife and my mother. I knew he and my aunt had lost an infant son about the time I was born, and maybe I reminded him of that boy, not in any known way or thinking way but in a way that was thicker than blood or water.

"Good-bye," I said. "I'll catch you again."

"Yeah," he said. "You do that."

Sleep

I SLEPT ONLY a few hours that night, tossing and turning in my bed, and what hours I did sleep brought me no rest. I thought on my going away and those thoughts were relentless. I wondered if I'd ever sleep with Afton again. That night it was all I cared about. It was all I wanted to do forever, to sleep with Afton, and yet so many of her ways I did not understand, and for lacking that I could burst to flame and ash away to nothing.

Moment by moment, my reckless mind was rising and falling to the occasion of life. I was constantly at odds with myself and the world and ill-fitted to my skin, and my brain was only dependable insofar as it delivered up half-thoughts, half-truths, jagged at the edges and more apt to spark fire and smoke than light and warmth.

There were no ideas like lanterns or small bright bulbs going off in my head. There were only beginnings, small blessings that kindled and flickered and disappeared in the blink of an eye. I could feel pain and desire and fear and longing, could feel my sweat drenching my skin, and this would not abate. I've discovered it to be my condition in life, a timeless consistency whereby I still live with everyone I ever lived with and still hate the few I have hated, am still afraid of what I've always been afraid of, still love whomever I've loved, still mistrust what I've mistrusted, which mostly means the stuff of myself.

It wasn't until it was time to get up that morning that the tiredness took its hold, but I had chores to do. It was nothing new. The need for sleep was always there on the farm. I've seen a man fall asleep perched on a stool, milking a cow, a man asleep on a tractor wandering across a field toward the river, with the plow dropped and nine furrows spiraling out behind. I've seen my grandmother sitting upright at the dining-room table and said the beginnings of a conversation, asked her a question, before I realized and backed away to leave her in sleep, and my mother doesn't now sleep at night but takes three or four naps a day.

I'd been lectured on sleep before, had been questioned by the old man on my mysterious and regular need for, say, five or six hours a night. I knew he took naps. He'd find chores for us to do and then he'd go in on the divan or the daybed on the piazza and rest his old head to gain strength so that he could come find you and chastise you for your apparent weakness, come find you and unleash a torrent of other chores that needed to be done.

"You were asleep," he'd yell.

"No, I wasn't," I'd say, the lie always preferable to giving in because to give in to him would deny him his argument and he'd then have to go straight to his lecture.

"I know you were sleeping," he'd say.

"No, I wasn't. I got hit in the head by something that came flying through the air. A big heavy thing that about killed me."

You could say stuff like that to him because most often he wasn't listening anyways.

"Sleeping, by God. Out tomcatting all night long. I used to drive down to Chesterfield in the buggy to see your grandmother and then I'd drive back and sleep in the barn until morning chores. Then I'd do it all over again the next night. Sleep? How the hell are you going to get anything done if you sleep all the time? If a man lived to be sixty and slept eight hours a day, he'd miss twenty years of his life. Man like that might as well stay awake and die at forty."

"I told you I got knocked unconscious by something flying through the air."

"What'd it look like?"

"I don't remember. It was going so hard it knocked the memory of itself right out of my brain."

"You expect me to believe that?"

"No."

"Well, maybe I do believe it. What if I did? I imagine you'd have a problem with that, too."

One thing I do know is the part about him courting my grandmother. She lived in Chesterfield and he'd drive his buggy down to see her every night. People I've asked say it's true, he really did sleep in the barn to be there for the milking.

Billy came with news that morning. A cross-country runner the academy had recruited was injured and taking a year off to rehabilitate, so Billy was going to get his scholarship. He'd be going to school after all. Tucker was trying hard to be happy for him while seeing his own plans to travel America snapped in two. He declared he'd be going anyway, only alone. It was clear how left out he felt, but this was all very good for Billy because in his heart of hearts he wanted to be an astronaut and to do that you had to be a pilot and go through the military. But to be a pilot you also had to be two inches taller than Billy was. He had his theories as to how he was going to pull it off, and I won't go into them here. They didn't make sense then and still don't Two inches is two inches, and it doesn't make any difference on which end you lack it.

Billy had predicted the moon landing and the space shuttle and Skylab. He could talk on about supersonic flight, astrodynamics, propulsion theory, astrogeology, astrobiology, thermodynamics, fluidics, life in the hypersonic range. When he got wound up and onto an astronaut jag, the words came out beautiful as story, beautiful unto themselves, and I had no need to understand them. It was enough to be in the presence of those words.

I grew up around men who worked, who possessed arcane and exotic languages, knew the names for all manner of things, things to be seen and things that could not be seen, like the interior of an engine or a cow, what was underneath the earth and overhead in the sky. What we were doing at any moment had its own name. It was called something and, by damn, you always had better know what you were doing. Sometimes those names were made up and often they were withheld, and the names could differ from man to man, so you had to know the man, too, and his way of naming. If you wanted to get in on the conversation, which was what it meant to be one of the grown-ups, you had to learn their language.

Later on, me and Billy will be in Texas and he won't be an astronaut; he'll be a lineman for a company that builds power lines. His hero will be Buckminster Fuller, and he'll be all knowing about Spaceship Earth and geodesic domes and how they form a hemispheric surface and what a savior technology will be. He'll tell me his dream is to build the first power line to the moon, and even though I was older and thinking of myself as pretty smart, he still didn't make sense to me. But I listened with rapture and challenged him so as to keep him talking through the long Texas nights.

WE STARTED INTO our painting and painted all morning, a mist of whiteness and whiteness and whiteness, and the barn took on its dressing and began to look the way it must have looked when it was first built, swabbed white, cow's blood mixed in that first homemade paint. It's rare to see now, but sometimes out in the countryside, on a back road late in the day, you catch the sun upside the wall of an old barn and swear you see pink, and it is the blood of long-dead cows that is so pretty in the light.

Tucker drove the loader, low-range, low-gear, finger-ing the levers to his side to raise and lower Billy in the bucket. There was a subtle breeze that morning, and when turned just so it caught the finer mists of the white com-ing out the nozzle at the end of the wand in Billy's hand, and without realizing it we were having ourselves painted white, too.

The barn took on its gallons of paint all that morning, down the long and across the high. The barn was built in the shape of a cross. At the long, it was one story and ran over a hundred yards where we walked the paint on. At the transverse, it rose to three stories and was sixty yards long, and it was slow going. I kept looking for a yellow ten-speed to come down the road. I hustled to keep the paint stirred and the reservoir full and the hose untangled, and Tucker crept along with Billy in the bucket, going up and down, sweeping his hand to cast white like a magician.

Tucker had a watermelon on ice in his van and was quite proud of it, bragged on it all the while, as if to say, Maybe Billy's scholarship did come through, but right now I've got something you all want, that watermelon. He looked fondly toward eating it at dinnertime, and he wanted us to watch him and envy him while he did it.

When we broke for lunch, my arms were slopped white and my face was speckled and my back and chest were splotched with paint. I wanted to talk to Afton, wanted to know if it was over and, if it was over, what had it been? I know I had no right to push such thoughts, to not be content and to not give room, but I needed to hold on to something. Tomorrow always seemed light-years away to me, yesterday always bumping at my back and then going distant.

We went to see Tucker's watermelon and found it'd already been cut in half, with the pink eaten out of it. Tucker blamed me and Billy, but he himself could vouch for our whereabouts. My mother and my grandmother had gone off for the day, leaving plates of meat loaf and corned beef sandwiches, bread and potato chips and butter pickles, deviled eggs and jugs of lemonade and iced coffee, which we had outside. I asked Billy if Carol knew he was going to school. She was a year behind us and he was very much in love with her, but she thought of him as a best friend. He seemed patient about that, held within himself the confidence that she'd come to look on him the same way he looked on her. He told me she was the first one he called and she was very happy for him.

"In a friendly sort of way," Tucker said. "You two are pathetic. Both whipped."

I told Tucker to kiss my ass and he did not think it was funny and I could see him thinking about coming at me, wanting to do it in the worst way, but I was a whole more than he'd want to tangle with and he knew it. So he lit a joint right there where anybody could see him. He was trying to push me. And also, if Tucker couldn't hurt the one he wanted to he'd hurt himself.

After that we went quiet for a time and ate our food and Tucker got over his spitefulness and then we cheered up and talked about whether or not we could kill ourselves and, if we talked about whether or not we could, how we'd do it. Tucker was a shotgun sort of person and

Billy went for drugs or crashing a jet into a mountain and I said I didn't know, so they began thinking up ways for me to kill myself.

I told how I remembered that tramps would come by when I was a kid. They'd be old men with satchels and maybe a dog. One old-timer rode a bicycle with fat tires and big, sweeping handlebars and passed this way two, three summers in a row. He did silhouettes with a pair of scissors. He'd do bears, cows, deer, cats, whatever you'd tell him. Chickens, roosters, birds, and not just your average dog but different breeds of dogs.

One time he made a cutout of the farm. It was four feet long, and you could see the house and the machine shed and the barn and the sawdust shed and the calf barns and the bull barn and the tenant houses. He gave it to me, but I always had to give him something back, something, anything—a quarter or a dime, a lock washer or a handful of split shot. It didn't matter. It was the idea of something for something.

"What happened to it?" Billy said.

"I don't know. Lost it, I guess."

"So what?" Tucker said. "So fucking what? Did he kill himself or something?"

Then the old man came walking from the barn, tapping his cane with style, walking all jauntylike, as if his feet were spring-loaded. I could tell he was about to make some money. He asked how the painting was going, said the white looked quite done to him and told Tucker to tell me to pull the cattle truck up to the loading chute and drive the marked cows onto it. They were headed south.

"I wonder what goes through their minds," Tucker said to him. "They're leaving to go."

"Well, I never did see one get homesick," the old man said, and then he said, "Is that my lunch? By Jesus, you ate my lunch."

"No, I didn't. He did," Tucker said, pointing at me. "He gave me his lunch and he ate yours."

"Well, one of you did, and I want to know which one."

That was when I knew it was the old man who ate the pink out of Tucker's watermelon.

I smiled at him and said, "Why, I thought you already ate."

He knew I'd figured him out on this one and he told Tucker to tell me to never mind about the truck, he'd do it himself when he had a free moment. Said it like I wasn't good enough to load his cows, said it like he was busier than God. He looked at his watch and up the road and said he had to be getting out of here, which was okay by me.

As soon as he was gone, we could hear the blasts of air horn to the north and then the building rumble of diesel, its knocking engine and the rolling on of a heavy cargo. An eighteen-wheeler chuffed in, loaded with hay out of Quebec. It was a delivery the old man had neglected to mention.

The window was down, and blaring out the opening, across the thick forearm of the driver, Vanesse, was the sound of Hank Snow, the Singing Ranger, and his Rainbow Ranch Boys: "I'm Movin' On" and "I Don't Hurt Anymore."

He blew the air horn again and got down from his rig all shy and sheepish, a stump of a man, thick and built low to the ground. He waved and yelled out my name and came over into the shade.

"You've been what?" he said. "You been painting? And then he laughed at us, painting being not such respectable work.

"Fuck this shit," Tucker said, staring at the tons and tons of hay.

We pulled in whomever we could find to help unload the hay, which wasn't too many because they'd also heard the trailer truck coming down the road. We got a crew, though—the ex-con and the milk-house boy, who was called that even though he was fifty-four, and Henry and Robb, two brothers who lived up at my uncle's farm.

Cy came over, too, and I told him he could get us some water jugs.

"Water, shit," he said, and walked away and didn't come back again that day, like fetching water was not such respectful work either.

Tucker and I climbed on the trailer with Vanesse, and everyone else went up into the loft. Vanesse wore a leather apron and we all had hooks. Making hay and selling it south was what the Vanesse family did. By morning he'd be parked in the fields up there in Quebec, asleep in the cab, and his brothers would be putting on another load, bound for Massachusetts or New York State.

We started in but didn't get far before the belt on the elevator began to slip. It'd already been through a hay season. It was old and stretched and began to lag on the pulley under the heavy and steady load of big Canadian bales. The spiked chain that moved the bales chattered and made a ratcheting sound as it skipped on the cog, so we stopped work and I replaced the belt and removed a link from the chain and reefed on the tightener. I was tired and careless and the wrench slipped and I barked my knuckles on the frame, skinning them up pretty good. I cursed and threw the wrench off into the bushes. Tucker and Vanesse laughed at me as I plucked away the skin I'd peeled back, and Tucker told me to go up in the loft where I'd be safe.

"Up there, it's only hot," he said.

I lumbered up the rattly skeleton of the hay elevator and told Billy and the other four I'd give them each twenty bucks to let me sleep. They laughed and agreed but wanted the money up front, so I pulled the bills from my jeans and gave them out, which surprised the hell out of them.

The bills were new and damp with sweat and carried ghostly stains of white paint. Billy, the ex-con, and the milk-house boy held them up and snapped them a couple times and stuffed them away, but Henry and Robb wouldn't take the money.

Down below, Tucker plugged in the elevator, and the spiked chain began clattering away again. Vanesse and Tucker started sending up the bales, and lulled by the noise, I fell asleep back in the bay on a bed of silky redtop we'd hayed off the low ground of a wet meadow on a hot day when the seeps had gone dry.

The clatter of the elevator and the conveyor in the loft set up an awful racket, but it was like sleep music to my brain, like fixing on and listening to your furnace on a winter's night, like the throb of an air conditioner in a motel room when you are alone and far from home.

It became sweet, tired sleep, and since that time I've slept in all manner of places, slept in rest stops beside the highway with and without a car, slept in the break room of a cotton mill within earshot of the rapid-fire shuttles and the din of the heddles. Slept in the desert, the snow, and the woods, on a riverbank, and, one winter night, in a churchyard in New Haven. Have slept in the back of a deuce and a half, rumbling through the outback of Texas.

When I awakened, it was in a world gone dark and silent. I held my hand close and touched my eyes to affirm their existence. I could not see a thing. I sat up and depended on my eyes to adjust, to find something and know what it was, but it didn't happen. I started feeling around, and it came to me that the bastards had buried me in the hay mow, surrounded me with bales. Underneath me, I could hear the cows snorting, could hear them at their water bowls, could hear the vacuum pump kick on, and knew it was four o'clock, time to milk. A moment later came the hiss of compressed air and then the slugging sound of the pulsators clipped to the tops of the milking machines, like heartbeats drawing milk instead of blood.

The cows were letting down their milk, and this would begin the slosh, swash, spatter, and burble of the late-day milking—milk going through the mammary system, down the udder and the teats and into the thin rubber hoses, into the stainless steel, into more black hoses, into the bulk tank so that people could have their milk and cheese and butter and ice cream.

I thought about Afton, like, What does food in her mouth taste like to her and how is the temperature of her body calibrated—as in, What is cold to her and what is hot? What is she like when she is alone, and when she thinks about me, how does she see me?

And then I remembered how, in that swale of wistful redtop, was a bale of hay with a snake in it, held down by the twine. Billy hooked the bale onto the wagon and that snake raised up its head and licked out at us with its red tongue and squirmed its tail. Snakes get baled up that way all the time, and once there was a fawn and another time a bird. In the winter, when you are shaking out the sheaves of hay, you can find the tiny bones of field mice and squirrels and moles.

I started climbing. I climbed to the collar beams where the vents were, and the rising and exiting heat created a towering draft. Dust and chaff swirled in the cracks of light, and invisible spores occupied the air, filled my mouth and nose. I climbed up the well of hay they'd left, to where the swallows lived, and knocked aside a bale. There was light, and instead of making for the door or one of the chutes, I turned and crawled along inside the peak, with the ridge board at my back and the points of nails come through the roofing, and made for the window on the gable end, desperate for the cool air I could feel coming from that direction. To the window side, I could hear the honeyed sound of doves purling forth. These were doves who lived in the loft, a pair I depended on at odd times to make their presence known to me.

At the window, I looked down and could see Tucker and Billy lolling in the grass at the edge of the drive, drinking beer and sucking away at the cool rinds of the leftover melon; could see bird shadows and cloud shadows, their dark traveling air marking the drive, passing unnoticed over Billy and Tucker.

I could also see from there the soaring vault of the sky, its blue swelter and sheets of sunlight, the warp of its thread visible and fanning and shooting down from the beam of the sun, and, way off, there was a wolf tree tottering on its stump. I could see where it would rain tomorrow, could feel it in this high air. I could see milkweed pods and tasseled corn, the fleshy bottomland forest and cattail marshes, and down by the river, the water-stained soil and the drift lines where small piles of debris lay to the flow of water. I could see the water-marked trees and, farther out, the forested land, dry and wet.

"You rotten bastards," I yelled down, and they started laughing and I did too. They laughed so hard they snorted beer and slapped their thighs. This was when Tucker's brother Alvin and his friend Butch showed up, and I couldn't help what happened next.

Alvin was not happy. He had not appreciated what all Tucker had done with that saw, claimed Tucker had absconded with some of his belongings. He just walked up to Tucker, held out his hand, and when Tucker went to take it, sucker-punched him with the other one. Billy stood and assumed the posture of an old-timey fighter, his elbows cocked and his fists raised. Butch picked him up and dropped him on the ground and sat on him.

Alvin drove Tucker's head into the drive, which was hard as concrete, and kept on from there, and Tucker just took his blows and would not hit back at his brother.

From the distance, the blows seemed to come without violence and the fight seemed dull and tired and without heart, without people involved. Alvin was not a cool and focused puncher, and it was not a fight anyway but a beating. He'd swing upward, and I could imagine the sting, the thud, and then the dull to sharp pain down through the body. They were staggering, getting tired from giving out pain and from taking it.

I thought that Alvin wasn't hitting his brother so much as he was laying hands on the world. He was wanting to send out messages, to make declarations like: Don't fuck with me and I'm so fucked up and This isn't the way it was supposed to be.

I closed my eyes and wished to be blind but could still hear moans and the sound of fists on flesh and mouth and head and so wished to be deaf, hardened deaf, and then I began to crawl. The roofing nails ripped my clothes and scratched at my back, and by the time I crawled out Alvin and Butch were gone.

I was for going after them, but how do you say that to someone's brother? So I said, "Jesus, Tucker, what are you going to do?" and he tried to smile, looked at me, and spat some blood. He didn't look too bad. The swelling hadn't started yet, but when it did his face would blossom and his body would be a rack of pain.

"I guess the joke's on me," Tucker said, and that was it. He collected himself up, and he and Billy headed for the van.

That night, I finished my supper and was playing an endless game of solitaire at the kitchen table. I was wanting and waiting for the phone to ring, to hear from Billy as to how Tucker was and, more so, wanting for it to be her.

My father was asleep in the chair and Billy Graham was in Liberia or Phoenix or some such place where people needed to be soul-saved. My mother had gathered up my aunt and my grandmother to the television to hear the music and to watch him save those people as they streamed in from the bleachers, the look of ecstasy and transport on their faces.

I wondered if Tucker could use some churchgoing, leastwise someone as big as God to tell him what to do. He had taken an awful thrashing at the hands of his brother. I had never seen such a fight before. It went beyond what I had seen in the way of people doing damage to each other.

There were other fights in my life, but two I remember the most. After my mother and father got married, the old man gave them an acre of land. They built a house on that land, this house, and during those early years my father worked nights on the farm to make the extra money to afford it. One night I was there with my father, helping him load ensilage to feed the cows. Afterwards we went into the milk house to wash up and he got to joking around with Cy. Both were younger and full of muscle, and one thing led to another. My father got him down and Cy's shirt was ripped across the back. My father helped him up, took off his own shirt and gave it to Cy, made him take it and told him he was sorry. After that, Cy started coming up to the house and they'd drink my father's home brew down in the cellar.

The other fight was on a New Year's Eve. A car pulled into our driveway and my father went out to see who it was. He was bent down talking to the driver. I was watching out the kitchen window when my father's head suddenly snapped back and a man came out of the car and punched him again and again. My father'd been drinking, so couldn't put up much of a fight, and the man had him down and was pounding on him. My mother had been watching, too, and she screamed, and my brother ran for his gun. When I opened the door to run out, our dog, a German shepherd named Bullet, took off out the door and got the man by the leg. My mother ended up in the middle, trying to call off the dog, trying to make the man stop, and trying to keep my brother from shooting him in the head to make him stop. I was a little kid. I didn't know what it was all about and still don't and don't really want to. I do know my brother should be proud for what he was willing to do.

After the man left, my mother got my father into the house. His nose was bleeding all down the front of his face and shirt, and his lips were smashed. I don't know where my brother went. He must have disappeared for a while to be alone. My father passed me in the hall and looked down at me, blood gumming his mouth, and said, "What's the matter? You never been in a fight?"

I backed away and he punched me in the stomach.

My kings were up and my aces set over to my right on the kitchen table. I knew what cards lay facedown, knew

I would win this game, could most often tell whether I'd win or lose long before game's end. I collected the cards and shuffled the deck, set it down on the table with a snap.

I took a drink from the faucet and woke up my father and asked if he remembered the silhouettist who used to come around on his bicycle.

"That old fool," he mumbled.

"Did you ever hear that he killed himself, or is that made up?"

"What's the difference," he said, carelessly, off-handedly, as if to end a long and casual conversation between us, wanting nothing more than to go back to sleep.

These were small bursts in the years of days. Most days were full of nothing, nothing at all; time weighed, got marked, and moved on. These were the days when I composed in my head, sought to make something be.

The phone rang and it was Afton. She wanted to know if I was okay, told me she'd been worried about me, and we both seemed to understand that I was to be worried over. She asked me if I still wanted to go to the fair on Friday night, a date sort of thing, out in public.

I told her, Sure, but that I didn't know if I could live that long without her. I might die. She told me to try, and I could see her smiling. She told me to buy some Life Savers, and before I could reply, the phone went dead, as it was sometimes wont to do, and I could only hang up and curse. Then the lights went out, too.

Outside, I could see across the hollow where the lights had gone out at the farm, so I dressed and hiked on down. The old man was standing there waiting as if he knew I'd be along shortly. I backed a tractor up to the auxiliary generator and attached the PTO. I wound up the rpm's, and the old man threw a switch in the house. There was light, there was power for the pump and power for the bulk tank to keep the tons of milk stirred and cold.

"Thanks," he said, and shuffled back to the house.

I filled five-gallon cans with diesel and topped off the tractor's fuel tank. My uncle showed about then, coming down from his farm in Walpole. He walked through the barns to make sure everything was okay and told me there was a storm coming down the river and the power was out all over the countryside.

"You got it under control here?" he asked me, and I told him I did. He nodded and drove off to check the heifers in the fields. Sometimes he drove all night from pasture to pasture to make sure the fences were strong and holding, to count heads and then swing home for a little shut-eye. I crossed to the house and settled into the hammock for the rest of the night, lulled by the noise of the tractor, fully able to come awake if the noise should stop. Some hours later, power was restored.

Earth

IT WAS THE morning of another day in the last days of summer. Small trees in leaf swayed in the fresh, unsummer breeze, and on the river and the lake there were crested wavelets, frothing and disappearing and rising and cresting again. At first the water must have looked hand-swept, but in some hours the breeze got stronger and large branches went to moving, and as the day wore on whole trees would go to motion and it'd be hard to walk against the wind. It would come to rain that day, a lashing, dinning rain, and we had the gable ends to finish and were to start on the black of the hundred window casings, but not this day. This was an autumn day, leastwise the messenger of autumn.

I rode the tractor at sunrise, a slicker bunched under my seat. The wind dressed down the trees, and the air had a touch I hadn't felt since the last season between spring and summer, when the days were warm, days that melted away the snow in the woods and the nights were cold enough to freeze what had melted.

The hair on my arms stood to the wind and my body closed itself to the breeze, then opened again to the calm, the weight, the density of the air. I stopped at the edge of fallow ground, a flight of land next up from the river, and geared down and engaged the PTO. As I eased ahead and the chain began to roll and the beaters spun, the manure flew skyward in a grand rooster tail.

By field's end I'd run out the load and could see deer at the forest's edge. They weren't frightened. Most people can look right at a deer and not see it, because they are looking for a deer, a whole deer, maybe a color they think a deer would be; but what to look for is the line of a deer, the horizontal of its back. The birds and animals, they live at the edge where cover meets cover: crops, woods, brush, grass, and water. One for refuge and one for resource, and when they move, they move at the edges of time, at dusk and dawn, to enter the open, to cross the open, to graze and hunt and forage and return again to the cover.

Tucker and Billy showed that morning as I was finishing up my breakfast and telling my grandmother how good it was and how I loved her apple pies. She saying, Well then, I just might have to bake one.

Tucker didn't look too hot. One eye was swollen shut and he had his nose packed with cotton. In general his face looked like it was some kind of vegetable, like an eggplant or a squash that someone had gone after with a belt sander and a paring knife. That's how his face looked, and of course his disposition was inclined in the same direction. Billy and I went inside for a cup of coffee while Tucker stayed on the porch watching the weather, seeming to enjoy what was brewing, seeming to enjoy his badges of pain.

"Afterwards," Billy said, "Tucker got his rifle and we drove around looking for Alvin and Butch."

"Do you think he'd've shot him?' I said.

"I don't know. He was pretty pissed. He said he was going to kill him. Look, we're going to work the day like we said and then I think we should head out. I'll get him west and then hitch back. There's nothing here for him and there could be problems if he stays around."

The lights in the house dimmed and went out and then came back full. Somewhere this storm was raising hell and would be on us in a little while. I told Billy again how happy I was for him that his scholarship had come through. He told me he hadn't been running much and was worried about what kind of shape he was in. The only running he'd been doing was running around with Tucker.

"So what did Carol say?" I asked him.

"She had some news of her own. She's getting engaged."

"You knew it was coming."

"Is that like an I-told-you-so kind of thing?"

"Well, you did."

"You gotta have faith," he said, and I thought the words over to myself. You gotta have faith.

We finished our coffee and went out to the porch. The old man was there talking to Tucker.

He was saying, "By the Jaysus, one day I got hit by

lightning four times while I was planting corn. First it'd hit one marker arm on the planter and then the other. The lightning hit those arms and it traveled through my body every time, and that was just the morning."

"Well, you've got to remember," Tucker said, "you are some kind of fucking god. That'd kill a normal man."

"Well, I was younger back then and I could take it."

"I bet that lightning turned that seed corn into popcorn. Is that what happened?"

"No, it didn't. How the hell are you going to turn seed corn into popcorn? It's another kind of seed altogether."

"That's right."

"But I bet you it could've if I'd had popcorn seed."

"Is there a point to this? Are you trying to tell me something?"

"Yeah, you don't go home every time the sun goes behind a cloud."

That day he put us to cleaning cows, brushing them down and combing out their tails, and then we were to clean the calf pens and haul in new bedding and sweep away all the cobwebs, as if the aerial photograph would be an X ray.

All day the old man watched us and hounded us. He carried a milk stool with him so that he could sit and talk and watch over us at our work, make sure it was done the right way, but not just the right way, the best right way—the best right way to shovel shit and sawdust, the best right way to tie a knot and fold a tarp, the best right way to stack and heave and walk and hold your head on your shoulders.

He tormented us with his opinions: how nobody wanted to work anymore and that's what was wrong with the country, and how there was going to be another Great Depression, and how the government was going to call in all the money and reissue new money as a means of stealing hidden, unaccounted cash, and how he didn't understand what Negroes wanted, and how cigarettes were bad for you, like poison, and ice water wasn't good for you either, and how he didn't like long hair or beards on men, and how you shouldn't sleep with anyone you didn't want to sit across the breakfast table from.

He pestered us with questions about people we didn't know he even knew and with questions about people we'd never heard of before. Complained how nobody minded their own business anymore. Wanted to know about various drugs and what they did for you, wanted to know if pot was something you could just buy and what it did to you.

"I like the white," he said, "but you can't have an all-white barn. You've got to have some black on it. Goddamnit, don't lift with your back; lift with your legs."

"Yes," Tucker said, grunting as he heaved a forkful of sodden bedding out the window into the spreader. "Got to have some black in it."

The old man sat by the open door to get the breeze while we mucked out the pen. He smoked a cigar and tapped at the concrete with his cane. The calves stayed together, circling the walls as we worked. The pen hadn't been cleaned in some time and smelled sharply of ferment and ammonia, a high-in-the-nose kind of smell that nails you in the forehead and makes your stomach churn. The cigar smoke drifting from the open door was sweet and pleasant.

When we finished bedding the pen, the old man had us follow him to behind the barn, where he had a stone he wanted us to move. He already had the pickup backed in and our job was to lift the stone onto the bed of the truck. It was a squared stone, five feet long and two foot by two foot, with a hole drilled through the center lengthwise. A stone like that weighs close to a thousand pounds. He wanted the stone taken up to my uncle's farm, where he had a new team of oxen to play with.

"I'll get the loader," I said.

"Nah," he yelled. "You don't need any g.d. loader. I'm going to teach you something you won't forget, but you can't tell anyone because then they'll know, too."

After lifting the stone, we moved to the calf pen off the grain room. Billy went on and on about how smart a way it was for us to lift the stone, just three of us, and how the old man was brilliant. He went on about how it made the pyramids seem not so inconceivable, and Easter Island, Stonehenge, and all such monuments attributed to beings from outer space, until finally Tucker told him to just shut up about it.

Outside, the rain came, and it was wind-driven, drumming the walls, coming to earth in slants and swirls, then going quiet, then lashing out again. It was desperate and reckless on the wind and wouldn't last the day. I thought about Afton sitting on her grandmother's porch overlooking the lake, deep in thought about no small things, maybe reading a book or writing a letter.

The old man came back, came strolling like it was a sunny day, and took up where he left off. He was flattered with Billy's wonderings on how his mind worked to figure out the moving of the stone, but not for long. It wasn't the way to be around the old man. To talk at him was a quick trip in the direction of his closing you out. If you were a talker, he didn't like to trust you.

"You ought to stay right here," he said to Tucker, "and work for me."

"How'd you unload that stone?" Billy asked.

"And why should I do that?" Tucker said.

"These two are going away. What are you going to do? I need a partner, someone to teach the business to. Everything a body needs is right here—milk, meat, vegetables. You work hard, you'll have something."

"I don't think so. Whole big world out there to see."

"Whole big world to get stuck in your face. People go away, they never come back."

"Moving that stone was amazing," Billy said.

"Up yours," Tucker said.

"Be that way, mister. You mark my words though," the old man said.

"You know," Tucker said, "that stave silo is a real eyesore, not to mention a hazard. You ought to have it taken down before you get your picture taken. If it were my picture, I wouldn't want that silo in it.

The old man pulled at his chin and gave his cigar another suck. Silo, shit, he said, and hustled off through the puddles to look at the silo, plagued by the idea Tucker had placed in his head.

"Time for a smoke, Tucker said, and we gathered out-doors under the eaves in the wet, cooling air. We were spattered with shit and our pants were soaked to the knees, but outside was the smell of sawdust and hay and turned earth and the deep blanket smell of the cows and, faintly, sour milk dumped away from the strip buckets.

"Moving that stone really was something. It's now so obvious," Billy said.

"Would you give it a rest?" Tucker said.

I pondered the way Tucker could get inside the old man's brain. They were so unlike each other except for their notions of independence. Tucker was a curiosity to the old man, someone he'd yet to learn and so could not contain, and for all his griping, Tucker liked the old man immensely.

"Look," Billy said, and from where we were we could see the old man at the silo, his posture set as if he were sizing it up and about to take it down himself, wondering only how fast to run and where to hit it and with which shoulder. The rain drizzled from the dark, close sky and he stood it like he didn't care, like he didn't even know.

"He's the god, all right," Tucker said. "The goddamned."

Coming out of the hollow a procession of machin-ery could be heard. It was the county farm. They'd fin-ished their haying and were bringing in the equipment. There were tractors with baler, rake, sickle-bar mower, and a conditioner, and wagons with the last of the hay they'd left from the day before. Gangs of men were piled on top of the wet loads, their heads ducked under the weather. They didn't say anything, didn't yell out.

They only stared, and I wondered what their lives must be like under the control of men who left hay to get rained on.

When the caravan had passed out of sight, the weather broke on us again. They had five long miles to go before reaching dry cover. I wondered what they would do with all that wet hay. I trusted they'd get those bales spread out and salt them and let them dry and break out the wettest to feed. But how to trust those in charge of those who can't be trusted?

We ducked back inside the doorway and could see the old man going off in the direction of the house and were relieved he didn't come our way. By and by, a state trooper car pulled in and two troopers got out and Tucker whispered, "Holy shit," and got us to boost him up through the ceiling into the low attic where the rats lived.

Billy said he'd take care of it and went out to talk to them. I could see him shrugging and looking off, and them pointing to the van, and him shrugging again and then going over to it and letting them poke around inside. They came up with a .22 rifle. The old man came out and shooed Billy away and spoke to the troopers until finally they took the .22 rifle and left.

"What's that all about?" I said.

"Well, last night, remember when I said how Tucker couldn't find his brother to shoot? He started shooting out insulators on telephone poles and power poles and blacked out most of the town."

"What's the old man sticking his nose in for?"

"I don't know, but I think it's as good a time as any to

get our stuff together and get down the road. If I get him west, out of state, it'll just blow over after a time."

Tucker dropped down from the ceiling. He touched at his red-and-purple face as if it'd just started hurting all over again.

I went to the house and found the old man on the phone. Phones were something he never fully understood. He'd nod his head or shrug and then after a silence he'd say, I just said no, didn't I? or, I told you I would, like the person on the other end could see him. He preferred you to stand when you talked on the phone, so you wouldn't get long-winded.

When he was done I told him how Billy and Tucker were taking off and wanted their checks and maybe he should give them a little bonus.

"Look," I said. "They worked hard all summer and stayed out of trouble and got your hay in. Maybe you could give them something extra."

"I imagine you already told them I would. Already spent my money for me."

I didn't say anything.

"You did. By the Jaysus, you're spending my money. You want them to have a bonus, you give it to them. The idea of paying someone extra for doing what they agreed to cuts no ice with me. Besides, they're leaving before the job is done."

"Well, maybe I'll do the same."

"Go then, if that's what you want."

I should've gone, but what would it have proven? I took Tucker and Billy their checks. We said to each other,

"See you around," "Yeah, see you around." Tucker smiled and told me I could have the rest of the beer stashed in the woods, and that was it. They were gone.

I did see Billy that year at Christmastime, and what the academy had done to him was frightening. It was like they'd snuffed out a flame, like they'd turned that flame on its source and made the two scared of each other. Tucker came through town that Christmas, too, and we talked about kidnapping Billy, and then Tucker moved on again. Billy lasted some months at the academy before he left and came back to be his old self and found work. We were in touch through to the last days we spent together down in Texas.

A long time later, Tucker got shot and killed. He was walking into the front door of the mobile home where he lived with his girlfriend, and she was standing inside with a pistol. It was his pistol she was holding. He'd hidden it in pieces, the gun, bullets, and clip stashed in different places around the mobile home to keep them away from the children. They had two boys—one was three years old and the other was two—and a six-month-old baby girl. His girlfriend shot him once and hit him in the right side of his head and then she left.

When they found him, he was lying on the front steps. He died within minutes, and they say he was never coherent enough to know where he was or what had happened to him. In the morning, when everything was said and done, he'd left a five-foot-long blood stain, and there was blood on the wooden stoop and the black iron steps lead-ing up to the door, along with a laceless black-and-white high-top sneaker.

He'd come back to work on the old man's farm. He'd mellowed out, as they say, gotten to be like old wine or bourbon whiskey. He'd given up chewing at the world, being its antagonist, had recanted his old ways and had been attending church now and then. People said he was a good guy, he'd give you the shirt off his back; she could have shot him in the arm or the leg if she wanted to get him out of there; she didn't seem upset; he'd bend over backwards to help somebody; he was a hardworking, pleasant man who didn't drink and was devoted to his children; he would do anything for anybody; she didn't have to kill him; I had a feeling: this is dreadful.

I'd had occasion to ask that state trooper what my grandfather said to him that day about Tucker, the day they left, the day we moved the stone, and he told me the old man said that Tucker and Billy had spent the night right there on the farm and there was no way those boys could have done what they did. He told me my grandfather was a great man, he'd known him for a long time, and my grandfather had cosigned a loan years ago so he could buy his first house. Said, "He was like a father to me."

And when Billy died? Say there are things you have to live with, like the death of dreams and of those pure few who harbor them to the end, and when you get alone and a little tired and darkness has fallen, the memory of them comes over you like a sheet or a wave. They are like water returning into your body, the slow ineluctable movement of water, and before you know it you are sitting in a chair with all the lights off and you are crying like a fool and it is and isn't because of that death, but you pin it wholly on that death and it becomes the death of everyone you know, the death of everything. That's how Billy's death will always be to me. It was an event that made me wonder how much longer I had and always conclude that, no matter how much time, it didn't make much difference.

Stay Here with Me

THE NIGHT TUCKER and Billy left I was sitting at the dining-room table in my grandfather's house. It's the first room you enter when you come into his house, and the table in that room is a trestle table, big enough for twelve people to eat at. His chair wasn't at the head of the table but at the center of one side, and from there he could see out the tall, double-hung, eight-pane windows along two walls. He could see most of what was his, and when he wasn't eating or looking out the windows, he'd slide over to a rocker he had by the woodstove, prop his feet on the hearth, smoke a cigar, and enjoy his mind.

He asked me if I knew anything about someone's driving off into the corn up at the other farm a few nights back and he asked me if I'd heard the weather for the weekend. I told him I'd heard the weather was to be rain through to Sunday, the whole of Sunday. There'd be no sun on Sunday.

I told him this, though I had not heard and did not know from Adam the future of weather in any way.

"Sunday will be clear and beautiful," he said, rolling his cigar. "There will be a light rain on Saturday night to wet everything down so when the sun comes out on Sunday everything will sparkle."

I couldn't tell if he was predicting the weather or conjuring it. I'd been around him enough to mistrust him when it came to human limitations.

I sat at the table eating hash and eggs and fried potatoes. My mother and my grandmother were off at church, a summer service, praying on behalf of the men and boys in their lives, or maybe at a potluck dinner at the town hall, something to dress up for and later regret having attended and then decide wasn't so bad after all.

That night, the old man was tired from telling us what to do all day. He finished eating and stood and unbuttoned his trousers to reach inside to rearrange his balls. He hiked his pants back up and cinched them shut and sat down in his rocker.

From that rocker he could also tell time, could tell the progress of the chores and who was doing what. He could tell by the sounds outside—this tractor or that tractor, each engine having its own voice—and by the opening and closing of doors. The almost imperceptible dimmings of the lights told him what task was being accomplished, and by the pump in the cellar he could say, They need their hay, or They need their hay swept in, or They need their hay swept in again, or They'll be on their water soon, and within a minute you'd hear the pump kick on.

The farm is a place of unchange, slow and impalpable change, the tending of animals not so different now from what it was ten thousand years ago. Wherever I am in the world, I know what they are doing on the farm. It's how I am both set free and anchored in time, moored with a long line. I didn't learn to read a watch or a clock until I was fourteen years old. There was no need to learn such a thing. Even now I often have to think as to what year it is and can't remember dates of birth and death and holiday, and my feel for my time, this half of this century, is of dramatic time, not calendar time, and dramatic time is only story time, which is to say, time outside of time, timeless time, time forever.

I asked the old man why he kept doing that—reaching into his pants the way he did. He stood up and did it again, as if I'd reminded him, and then he crossed the room and at the dry sink found his box of Dexters, thumbed the cellophane from one and touched it up with a matchstick he struck on the seat of his pants. He got his fedora and put it on his head and took up his cane. He was ready to sit in his rocker again and go back to enjoying his mind. He enjoyed his mind better than anyone I ever knew.

He finally said to me, "Because I might not have them for very long."

I didn't say anything. What can you say when someone tells you such a thing?

"Now," he said, "if a man earned a hundred and twenty-five dollars a week and he deposited a hundred dollars a week in the bank, he'd have a hundred thousand dollars in ten years."

I kept eating, kept my mouth full so that I would not be tempted to talk.

"What would he live on?" I said. "Twenty-five dollars a week?"

"That's enough."

"Where would he live?"

"Live right here with me."

"I imagine."

"You stay here with me."

"I can't do that," I said, and I thought, You're going away, too. You're going away forever.

"In less than twenty-five years you'd have a half million dollars in the bank. By God, you'd be making thirty thousand dollars a year in interest alone and I wouldn't have to pay you anymore. You wouldn't even be forty years old."

"You figure that all out in your head?"

He didn't answer me. He smoked for a while and rubbed his temple, gone back to amortizing in his head, ciphering the payout of long-term interest. Then he asked how my father was doing, asked if he was drinking much or if he'd gotten some control over it, said he hadn't been around in a while and he'd sure like to see him.

As soon as I'd begin to say my father was this way or that way, the thoughts would fade away from my mind. My father. He slept. He used to drink quarts of Black Label and now he snuck cheap vodka. He got the shakes and the night sweats and sat in the house in his coat and hat, even in the summer heat. After he ate, he cleaned his teeth with a matchbook cover. Sometimes now I go to the liquor store for a bottle of wine or liquor and find myself wandering the aisles, looking at the bottles and jugs, and I think, He drank that and he drank that, and I smile with memory of him and leave without remembering to buy anything.

"He's a good boy," the old man said into the air. At first I didn't know whom he was talking about and then I realized he was talking about my own father.

Another thing he said, later on when Afton's father killed himself, was, He must've had a lot more courage than the rest of us. He was the only one I know to say such a thing, and by that time he was far, far gone in the withering possession of the cancer.

That night, a look came to his face like he'd seen the devil himself, like there was a red dog come burning out of hell and it was behind me, over my shoulder. The old man bolted from his rocker and beat feet for the parlor, leaving a trail of cigar smoke in his wake. Then I heard a knock and turned around. Charley Dickard was at the door. He had a scraggly black beard and the skin around his eyes was the color of gunpowder and he had a tiny cross tattooed into his forehead at the hairline.

He said he wanted to come in. He wanted a cigarette. He wanted to know if he could sleep in the bus. He'd just been released from the county farm and was walking to Keene but was afraid he was going to get killed because he kept finding himself walking down the middle of the road.

"Well, then, don't do that," I said through the screen door. "Don't walk down the middle of the road."

He acted like it was an idea to consider, not walking down the middle of the road in the dark of night.

"Where's the old man," he yelled. "I've got to see him."

We hadn't seen Charley Dickard in months. He was one of the strays the old man showed up with from time to time. Charley Dickard and his partner, Thaddeus, were to cut cordwood during the winter, stack it in long rows in the forest. After the snow was out, we'd move in and buzz it up to sell.

Charley Dickard and Thaddeus came better equipped than most. They had their own clothes, they had a tent and chain saws, and they were prepared to live there in the forest like pioneers, like lumberjacks, like hearty souls, like Henry David Thoreau.

They'd make the old man richer come a year, and he'd give them a cut. He told them all about depositing their money and how they'd be half millionaires in less than a quarter century, but that didn't last long. He got bored sitting in the woods watching them work and keeping their spirits up. One day they claimed someone stole their chain saws, so the old man lent them his crosscut and bucksaw, a bow saw and axes, and said, "By the Jaysus, them boys are going to cut wood like in the old-timey days."

He fired them up with a speech about the old-timey days, one I was audience to and had not had the pleasure of hearing before. But the old-timey days got old pretty fast, like most work does as the temperature drops and you do it long enough, and one morning at 4:30 I found them in the milk house, huddled around a space heater near froze to death and clapping life back into their bodies. They testified to having had visions as they almost died from the cold, visions of God and the Holy Ghost and God's son and black-winged creatures.

The old man was saddened by their failure and gave them another chance. He let them live in one of the tenant houses and shovel shit and brush cows, but he only needed one man. The way it worked was, he hired Charley, and as soon as he did that, Charley hired Thaddeus. Then Charley and the old man would sit and watch Thaddeus work not very hard, and the old man would say to Charley, You got a good man there; I just might have to hire him away from you. And Charley would say, Oh no, you can't do that; he's my number-one man.

A month later, another hired man, named Virgil, hurt his back and threw a fit all at once and moved out of the tenant house on the meadow, moved out on his wife, Dee Dee, and their little children. So Charley and Thaddeus moved into the house and Dee Dee's sister moved in, too, and my family made whispers about how terrible it all was, them laying around having sex whenever they felt like it. My uncle took the opportunity to hire someone reliable and moved him into the house where Charley and Thaddeus used to live.

Some days went by, and Virgil called the house to say he was coming back to get Dee Dee and the kids and take them off to Claremont. I was sent down the road to tell them he was coming and wondered what stage of lustful encounter I'd walk in on. I was disappointed to find them in their stocking feet but otherwise fully dressed.

I told them the news, and they let out a holler and pulled their gear together. Charley and Thaddeus were homeless again. I drove them off the meadow, and the old man found a broken-down school bus for them to live in. We dragged it onto the land where it couldn't be seen, cut a hole in the roof, and fitted it out with a woodstove.

I was often asked to recount what I'd seen when I went to get them, and no one was content until I agreed they'd all been down to scraps of torn underwear.

Then a private eye turned up to claim Thaddeus. Apparently his father and mother were big-time Boston psychiatrists and had had him institutionalized in all different places. In the process of switching from one nuthouse to another, he'd been set free while they were off in Europe. He hitched east out of Boston and hooked up with Charley Dickard in Worcester, Massachusetts.

After Thaddeus was carted away, that's when Charley went old-timey shithouse crazy. He began eating brewer's grain and drinking milk from cows' teats and reputedly having untoward relations with calves.

The old man told him, "Charley Dickard, you can't be doing that."

But Charley Dickard didn't listen, so the old man told him he'd fire him if he didn't stop, like that would make a difference.

Finally there was nothing to do but call in the Social Services, and when they came around to collect him up, Charley disappeared into the dark hay mow, where he made vile sounds, laughed some, and babbled like a maniac. I had to go up and get him and found him on his hands and knees, his eyes black and unblinking in the flashlight. He told me he would not come down unless the old man came up to get him. Told me they had a deal, a blood oath, promises to keep.

Now, I'd seen the old man handle a four-thousand-pound team of oxen, break them to his voice. Another time, a bull got loose, the last of the big bulls we ever kept, a leggy and slab-sided monster with a front end like a truck. It had already crushed one man's ribs, but the old man offered some grain from the barn window, and when that bull chuffed his nose into it, the old man snatched him by the ring, climbed through the window, and led that bull off to its pen gentle as a puppy.

It was people like Charley Dickard who scared him, who made him see the places in people he could not enter, so he told the Social Services people to stop their fucking around and to get their asses up there or he'd shoot Charley Dickard for trespassing. They called an ambulance and hauled him away to Mary Hitchcock Hospital in Hanover, where they hooked him up to all manner of devices to read his brain and determine what we already knew. Charley Dickard was crazy as a shit-house rat.

"Please let me in," Charley said. "Please let me in."

"Hey, Charley," I said, opening the door. "How are you doing?"

"Where's the old man?" he said.

"Charley, you still crazy?" I said. "If you're still crazy I don't think he wants to see you. That thing with the calves still gives him chills."

"Where's the old man?"

"He's hiding in the parlor. He doesn't want to see you here. He's having an aerial photograph taken of the farm, and I don't think he wants you around to be in the picture."

"I got to talk to him."

"You go, Charley. You better hit the road and keep to the shoulder."

"I need some smokes."

I gave him a fistful of cigars from the dry sink and he took them, scrutinizing them like King Kong checking out Fay Wray on the TV. They seemed to be what he wanted, so he turned off the porch and started for the road but then stopped and looked back to me.

"Matches," he said. "I need matches."

"No matches, Charley. I haven't got any matches for you."

"Hey," Charley said, "tell him I'm real sorry to hear he's got the cancer."

"Yeah, Charley. I'll tell him."

The old man came out, looking around comers, taking steps.

"What'd you tell him that for, tell him I was hiding? I could hear you from the other room."

He went into a tirade, fulminating on the state of the younger generation, the weak of mind and the infirm of spirit, mankind in general. Then, just as quickly, his denunciations receded or he simply got tired, and that was disappointing. I depended on his censures, his invective.

"Fuck it," he said. "What's it matter?"

"What about the past," I said, not believing my own ears. "What about the old-timey days, yester-evening and yester-morning. All that shit?"

And then he told me something like, Who cares? Most of that stuff's made up. You remember what you want to.

This is not how it was supposed to go. He was a rock of fury, a fuming windbag. What's a little cancer in the life of a dangerous god? It is so sad when people and things lose their edge.

"You've got that old-man smell," I said. "You're done for."

"You don't fuck with me, mister. You're walking on thin ice."

"I don't give a good goddamn if you've got cancer. I just don't care."

"Oh, now you're trying to hurt my feelings.'

"You stink like death."

That made him smile, and I could see him winding up to take a swipe at me, but there came a banging on the door. It was Charley again, and this time he opened the door of his own accord. He smiled when he saw the old man standing in the kitchen, and the old man looked to be haunted, looked on Charley as if he were an apparition come from the underworld to torment him in his days of dying.

"Have I come at a bad time?" Charley asked.

"What do you want now, Charley?" I said.

"It's raining."

"No, it isn't. It stopped a while ago. Look at the sky."

"It's wet out in the woods. Can I sleep in the bus?"

I told him an ex-con slept in the bus but he could sleep in the cab of a parts truck we had out behind the barn. Then, without thinking, I offered him a job helping with the painting. He said he'd take it, he needed work.

"Sorry to hear you got the cancer," he said, looking over my shoulder. He shrugged and left.

The old man pointed a finger at me and told me I was fired, said, "You're fired, mister."

"Who's going to get you ready for your goddamn aerial photograph?" I said, and then I told him I wanted a raise.

"What's the matter? You ain't been stopping up to the filling station lately?"

"I don't suppose that's any of your business."

This time the old man went berserk. He fired me again, disowned me, although I did not own anything. He denied my very existence, which I was already in the habit of questioning. It was a blistering attack. He gave me the speech about how everything he did was for his children and how he did nothing for himself and how what all he did for his children and his children's children went unappreciated by them and he was shit on by them and how he'd show us. His face went red and he blew a vessel in his eye and then another one, and for all that I was relieved.

When he finished his tirade, he huffed off to the piazza, where he slept in the summertime. I sat back down at the table in his place and collected up the newspaper and tried to read, but it wasn't long before my head was resting on it and I was asleep. Then came another knock at the door, and I thought it was Charley Dickard come back for something else. It was Afton in the window. She saw me look up, turned the doorknob, and quietly passed into the room.

"I was asleep," I said.

"I was awake," she said. "I thought one of us should be attending to the moon and the stars."

I smiled and I wanted to tell her as much, wanted to say thank you for I don't know what, but I was still mostly asleep and the words in my mind were like paints flowing into one another, ordering and reordering themselves, strokes of letters, daubs of syllables. She had materialized, come through the night to me, and, however unfair to her, I had long since imbued her with my own ideas of who she was, and would always be. Coming through the night, materializing, being all beautiful, all things—these acts confirmed my ideas.

"What are you doing here?" I said.

"I wanted to see if you were hungry, if you wanted to get a meal. Mostly I wanted to surprise you."

"I already ate. I can cook us something right here."

She stroked the blond wood of the table, looked at it as if it were an instrument, looked at it as if it were something new, something to do, her hands moving on the table where I had just eaten.

"No. I mean a meal. I want to sit in a restaurant and order food."

"Maybe we could go to Keene and get a pizza or a sandwich."

"No. I mean a meal. I want steak and a salad and a baked potato with sour cream and chives. Maybe a nice piece of fish."

"It's nine o'clock. Where will we find a place open?"

"I don't know. We could drive around until we do. Hell, it's only six o'clock in California."

"Hell, it's only three thousand miles. I don't think I'm dressed for it."

"Just put on some clean clothes."

"How did you get here?"

She gave me a funny look and I knew it was because she took my question in its most speculative, most abstract sense, like: How did any of us get here and where did we come from and what is our purpose, and all such questions that plague philosophers, crazy people, the high-minded, and the obstreperous. Then she smiled and told me she'd borrowed her grandmother's car. She flipped me the keys.

"Wash your face," she said. "You have newsprint all down one side." Then she slid a roll of peppermint Life Savers across the table, her idea of humor.

To the Fair

SITTING ON THE horse blanket I'd spread across the seat, we entered into that night in Afton's aunt's car, drove the back roads toward Keene on gas I had stolen from the pump. The land was about dry from a sowing wind that blew from someplace else where the world was rainless and warm, and it came to be that we were on our way to the fair for the late-night attractions, for the food, for the features.

I was dying to tell her how we moved the stone that day, dying to ask her why she was restless and could not sleep and was out and about and had come my way, and I wanted every answer to be about me, to edify, to illuminate, to bind us into one, but Afton turned cross before I spoke, and an edge came into her voice, a sad edge.

She told me she was tired of chatty people, aw-shucks people, and smart people, people in the know, people in

TO THE FAIR • 157

the news, people in general. She was tired of good guys and bad guys and feeling as if the whole world were closing in, as if she had invited the world and was now beset. She said she didn't know what she wanted in life or even what life was. She felt herself to be deliquescing.

I said, "What?"

"Deliquescing. Isn't that a beautiful word? *Deliquescing.*"

"What does it mean?"

"Dissolving, for some reason I forget."

"I can help," I said. "I can rub your back or something."

But she shook her head and said, "No, that's okay. It's chemical," and in the way she said it I knew I was somehow caught up in the way she was feeling. Somehow I was at the place of conflict within her.

"Why not?" I said. "I can help if I want."

"It's because you scare me."

"Oh God," I said, and I knew this is where we'd become just good friends or she'd say she loved me but wasn't *in* love with me.

"I worry over you. It's like I need to protect you all the time. Like you need me too much. Sometimes you hurt so damn much. There, I said it."

"Me?"

She slid closer and took my hand and told me how sometimes she was afraid of me, afraid that I was more in love with the idea of her than in love with her. I felt pinned and didn't know if I was pinned by the truth, though I was afraid I might be. My mind went chain-driven and I wondered how I loved, in what way did I do that.

All the while she'd been cross because she had stuff to tell me. She was the air before the storm and I was the earth she'd been softening up for news about myself, but it wasn't how I saw myself. I saw myself as solid and loyal, constant, true, steady, faithful, resolute, staunch, eternal, endless, but just then I saw it all differently, and this new way came out more like: continual. relentless, stubborn, interminable, unending, true to a fault, cold at the bone, raw of flesh, and brittle, weak at the edges.

I did the only thing I could. I told her it wasn't true that I didn't love her and I told her I didn't like her for implying those other things about me. I wanted to say, Why can't you see me how I really am? but knew it'd come out sounding like, Why can't you be the way I want you to be?

She said, "I'm not all that together myself, you know. Sometimes it's like I'm hanging on by the skin of my teeth."

Then she got up on her knees and put her face in my neck and her mouth was on my shoulder and I had the smart thought that she'd been talking about herself as much as she'd been talking about me. It's not so strange how we were drawn together. I wanted to say, I am not a person but a place for you. I too am outside looking in, and I cannot help myself either.

And to say, We are children of our times, children who have atomic dreams, children who witnessed the gunning down of all those famous men and those soldiers and students and marchers. To say, We are children of our families, nuclear and white and of a class and afflicted. To say that we are all the sum only of our parts. It takes no courage to think that way, to close in and draw down, to cut and cut lower, to let life be dwindled away to its parts.

She came even closer, and I had a desire to smell her hair, to tangle my fingers in those fine strands, to get my fingers on her skin and through to her muscles, to have my presence felt inside her, to taste the skin of her teeth.

I told her as much, and she took my right hand and held it to her body, saying, "Here . . . and here . . . and here." To touch her each time in each place was a small drama with a beginning and an end and a memory. There was the feeling we'd come through fire or war and we were too tired to look back to see what it was and were content to be together, moving through the night as if it'd been agreed to a long time ago.

In silence we rode, taking a long cleansing from those moments of truth telling, of what was and wasn't said. We rode for miles in the direction of Keene, winding the back roads that squirreled through the forest and rattling over the plank bridges until we saw colored lights on the horizon in the tuck of the high night. Afton said, "What's that?" and at first I didn't know and then I told her it was the fair. She asked if we were still going to go, and I brightened up and told her, "Well, yes, we're going right now, going tonight."

I told her there was food galore at the fair and there was, even if it wasn't steak and what all she said she was hungry for. There was hot corn on the cob we slathered with butter. There were hamburgers and hot dogs and sausage with peppers and onions and french fries drenched in vinegar. There were pies and cookies and cotton candy and fried dough.

She bought food at the fair as if she were shopping at the grocery. She bought fudge and maple candy and food from the deep fryers that she asked to have wrapped in butcher paper so she could eat it later. We filled an onion sack, and later she hung it from a bamboo cane I won and carried it over her shoulder like a hobo.

We toured the dimly lit cattle barns and I told her of each of the breeds—Holsteins and Guernseys and Jerseys and Ayrshires and Brown Swiss—and told her, This is a yearling bull and this is a heifer and this is a dam and this a sire. It wasn't so many years back that I'd been one of those 4-H'ers tending my show cows, waiting for night to fall to walk hand in hand down the midday with another young female 4-H'er, say a horsewoman or a shepherdess or a cowgirl. Then a chaste kiss and sleeping alone among the lowing cattle, letting them blow snot and drool on my sleeping bag. Then awakening to the cold morning to feed and wash and groom the cattle, that kiss on my mind.

I told her all such and she looked at me strange, like she didn't understand, and I told her it was like a dog show, only with cows, and that other kids had sheep and chickens and horses, but you rode the horses.

"Yeah, horses you ride," she said, and punched me in the shoulder.

We wandered in the direction of yawping chickens and into the poultry sheds, watched them strut and preen and bent to see into their glassy eyes. I do not know my poultry, so we had fun reading the cards and copying down the names on a folded-up paper I had in my pocket and would later copy over into a journal book like this: *poultry—Crevecoeur Block Hen, New Hampshire Red, Phoenix Silver Cock, Plymouth Rock Buff Pullet, Rosecombs, Black-Tailed Reds, Hamburg Golden-Penciled Cockerel, Wyandotte Partridge Pullet, Java Blacks . . . rabbits at the fair last night—Holland Lops, Harlequins, Netherland Dwarfs, Flemish Giants, Silver Martens, Tans, and Satins and Polish . . . the sheep pens and the horse stalls. Sheep—Hampshires, Cheviots, Suffolks . . . goats— Alpine, LaMancha, Nubian, Toggenburg . . . There was a pen full of peacocks, but we could not get them to fan out their tails. Afton talked to the animals. Everybody talks to the animals.*

In the long buildings were displays for purposes of education and signs and slogans for new products and farm safety—LIGHTNING KILLS, WEAR GOGGLES, DON'T WORK TIRED!!! READ THE INSTRUCTIONS, DON'T REMOVE GUARDS AND SHIELDS—and for horticulture and woodworking and the home arts. *The death rate for agricultural workers is fifty-two for every hundred thousand workers, five times greater than all other industries averaged.*

There were 4-H displays on better udder health, and candle-making demonstrations, and a sheep-shawl demonstration by the 4-H sheep kids. We read about treatment for mastitis and how to detect heats for purposes of breeding: *restlessness and alertness, banding and erect ears, riding other cows and allowing another cow to ride, dirt marks on cow's side, roughed hair on tailhead and rump, frequent urination, head resting on another cow's back or loin, mucous discharge and a red swollen vulva, milk yield may decline or increase daily.*

We learned the symptoms of milk fever, and Afton said she usually felt some of that way most of the time. We laughed and then we sat on tractors and I showed her plows and told her the names for the coulters and cutters and chisel points and shears and leveling bar and moldboard.

I showed her a planter and told her how it was Jethro Tull—not the musician—who invented the seed drill almost three hundred years ago, sowing seeds in rows instead of broadcasting them by hand. I was full of information.

There was a display on what to do when the bomb came down, with the same poster we had in the barn outside the milk-house door. The print on our poster was small and fine and almost unreadable because fly droppings and spatters of feed and shit covered it within days of its being tacked on the wall. When we whitewashed the inside of the barn, it became just a white rectangle tacked on the wall.

She said, "My father was in the air force in Korea. He took aerial photographs and read them with maps so the men would know where to drop their bombs."

So we talked about how horrible and wrong it all was and what a fuck Nixon was, and said all manner of other things that people were saying at the time and, still, we knew it was not so simple, knew that evil and danger were manifest in all the gray areas.

We moved on to the legumes, to the timothy and red clover and blue ribbon alfalfa, to the fertilizers, more tractors, chain saws, and organs. Afton said, "Who wants to hear about somebody's canned goods? No more homespun. I can't take any more of this." Maple syrup, photography, and painting.

There were Rototillers and snowmobiles and stain removers and sets of knives that let you turn watermelons into pirate ships and radishes into roses. Those knives were so sharp they were almost illegal.

There were freezers for sale and one was full of ice cubes, including a cube that held a diamond, and you were invited to chonk on all the ice you wanted to find it. Afton told me she had been proposed to twice in her life, and I had to keep my mouth shut because if I opened it I'd have said, I'll marry you.

Then I did say it, and she looked at me and did not answer, did not say yes or no, and that way I only felt a little foolish.

At the edge of the lights near a parking lot was a mud hole, and people were drunk and high and dancing half-naked in circles, sending founts of beer into the strobes of sweeping headlights, founts of ash, arcs of ember. Boys were dancing with girls and girls were dancing with girls and we watched. I didn't know much of that giddy stuff. It wasn't how I was raised or how I decided to be. The farm was outside the world and so I lived outside the world, grew up outside the world, and, just as a practical matter, sometimes had to be out in the mud when I didn't want to be and so did not think of it as something I'd do if I had the choice.

We watched the people in the mud and did not talk about them. The people in the mud were settling down, beginning to preen and slicken their bodies with mud where there wasn't any yet. People were touching themselves and searching out the best mud and the audience was growing. A band of drunks who did not possess the true spirit of mudhood came along and started touching one of the mud girls, and a mud guy did not like that, so the police had to come.

We made our way back towards the lights, towards the sounds of the horse pull. The pull was the free-for-all and was going late. Two teams were still in, and there was a mountain of stone on the boat. One of the drivers was swinging his team to the hitch, and his sons held the evener.

The big horses, matched Percherons, were twenty-five hundred pounds each, and they made all that flesh and bone and muscle prance to the front of the load, now better than ten thousand pounds of weight. They stopped and backed and backed, and you could see the fire in their eyes, like small black doors opening to a furnace not unlike the one buried in the earth. Then the boys dropped the evener on the hook, and at the instant before the sound of steel on steel, the horses surged into their collars. Their muscles defined their flesh and they drove so hard, stretching and articulating their bodies, that it was as if they would spread open the earth beneath their feet and ride upon the fire that would pour forth. The father intoned his driving chant—*Eee-yip! Eee-yip! Eee-yip!*—and they drew out the distance, and everybody in the bleachers roared.

"God," Afton said, "I have never seen anything like that."

I had seen it all before, seen the steers pull and the oxen pull, and they always seemed so naked and raw, pulling out of fear and dumbness. But every time the big draft horses pulled, they did it with pleasure and lust. They pulled because they loved to pull, and I could feel it in my chest and legs.

Across the pit from us was the old man, in a white short-sleeve shirt and wearing his fedora. He was leaning on the fence, chewing on a cigar and tapping the bottom rail with his cane.

Another old man was talking into his ear, but he was looking at us, and when my eyes met his, he smiled and nodded and I did the same and then backed away. As we were leaving the horse pull, someone took my elbow. I turned and it was the man my grandfather had been talking to and he handed me a twenty and told me my grandfather thought I might need a little pin money.

I thanked him and we made for the midway, to where, overhead, the moths were swarming the colored lights, dampening and shadowing the tubes of greens and blues and reds and yellows. From loudspeakers came calliope music, and the carnies were calling in the fair-goers, looking to separate them from their coin, looking to hoodwink them, and many were pleased to oblige.

This was the late-night crowd, drunk and rowdy. The mud people had not hosed off and had come onto the midway, enjoying the distance from others their muddiness made for. You could hear the thump of the sledge, a resounding blow, and the whang of the bell, good for a stuffed animal.

We rode the tilt-a-whirl, felt that sweep of force like a strong, fast hand holding us urgently in place. Afton shepherded me through the door to the haunted house, showing me the way to go, and I let her, all the while keeping my eyes on the floor, where cracks of light made a path you could follow.

We stopped to see the women come out dressed in their dingy scanties, mere wisps of underwear. Some were young and thin, their skin white and blue and red in the convergent light, and some had age, had flesh enough to sell.

Men stood at the stage and watched as if paralyzed, and I would've, too, would've paid my money and watched those women if I'd had a few beers and was alone with some guys.

"That's pretty sad," I said, and she said something like, "Maybe they do it because they want to."

"I don't get you," I said.

"We have to think that," she said, "because otherwise it makes them not people. It makes us like people who know better for them than they know for themselves. Like look at that. See the scar."

I could see the red of a scar coming through powder low down on the belly of one of the women and said so.

"She had a cesarean. She had a baby. She's a mother."

It was something I would not have seen on my own. This woman, I would have seen only what she wanted me to see, something different, as opaque as frosted glass.

Then the woman looked right at us, picked us out in the crowd like she knew we were talking about her, like we knew her secret.

"I'm tired of where there are people," I said. "I want to be away from here."

THE NORTH CEMETERY was not just a cemetery to me. It was a playground a quarter mile from my house. I'd go down there to walk the wide stone walls and swing on the iron gate. It was the door to heaven by way of a quick dive in the direction of hell. It turned death to peace.

So when we left the fair and drove back towards the farm I took her there and, on the way, I saw my father's car parked at a turnoff beside the road. I thought to stop and would have if I'd been alone, but tonight I was feeling outside of the world. We walked the hilly ground, closed in by the heavy walls gently shrugged into place and quietly riding the land's contours. I pointed out the stones I knew—the dead generations of my mother's family, the soldier's stone embraced by the trunk of an elm, and, almost gone from sight, the spalling stones of men surrounded by their several wives and their infant dead, the stones wedged into the sunken ground, the grass shallow, its roots moist in the cool land. Some stones were obelisks and some were flat slate and some carried finials on top. The cemetery was the record of death in childbirth, in war, in the sweep of influenza in 1917, but left to be imagined were accident and old age and unnamed disease, heartbreak and debilitation and the work of one's own hand or the hand of another.

Afton and I walked the grounds in the dissolve of the night, under the fairish shadows of the butternut and beech and the shining sumac, silver in the moonlight. I told her how it was my father's car we had passed on the road, and she said, "Oh, Robert," and I thought I'd break with hearing her voice. For comfort I fixed my mind on the cemetery's beauty of sorrow and grief.

"Everything will be okay," she said, her words an echo, whispery across the echo of my mother's words, Everything will out in the end.

I think it is for all time to wonder about your place in life. You sit and see, away in the sky, the Pleiades, open stars clustering in constellation, enveloped in nebulosity. You wonder how far it is between you and them. Late at night in July 1969 I dozed off on the couch and came from sleep, alone, to watch a man walk on the moon. Strange how, rather than my mind going out there to him, it turned in and seated itself more deeply inside me. If I'd not been alone, I would have told how frightened I was at that very moment, frightened for all of us.

I wonder how far west Billy had gotten Tucker, how far from here, how far from the meeting place. On the mountain we could hear the coy dogs congregating somewhere near the meeting place, fighting over what they'd scavenged or just fighting to play, snapping at each other's flanks. I looked to Afton beside me At the fair there was another thing I learned. She was the kind of woman both men and women fall in love with. When people looked at us—the mud people, the strippers, the paralyzed men at the rail, the horsemen and horsewomen and carnies—when all those people looked at us, it was Afton they saw, and in their eyes was wonder and longing, and in that they were like me.

When I asked her about it, she told me it had always been that way for her and sometimes the attention had not been good, sometimes people were seeing what was not there. But it was in her walk and in her face. It was in the way she held her hands or moved her arms, the way she spoke, lingering over her words. It had made her careful in life, because she seldom knew who she was in the eyes of others.

The dampness had left the ground and it had come to be warm earth in the cemetery. I unfolded the horse blanket and she lay down like a dead woman, east to west, and then she sat up and lifted her T-shirt over her head and unhooked her bra and shrugged it off her shoulders, and then she lay back and unsnapped her shorts and hunched her hips and shucked off her shorts and her underpants in one long, smooth motion and looked up at me.

"You seem bigger in the cemetery, taller," she said. "You get bigger and smaller like you're drinking the same stuff Alice drank to go down the rabbit hole."

I remember how white her skin was in that bay of silver light she'd found for herself. She was a sight come to me to be seen by me. I wondered what it must be like to wear her skin, to have her hair, to be able to smile the way she did and have eyes that held you like soft hands, to always be as near to her as she was to herself.

The moon banked more light off its hull, and where she was lit up she glowed as if the earth were fired with light. I lay down and across the river a freight train was going north and we listened to it make its rumble through the night like a long wind in the hollow, traveling over the brook. I began to fade with tiredness, and though it was the last thing I wanted to do, I went to faraway sleep lying next to her nakedness, tired from the day and night. And when I woke up, she was shaking me. Her fingertips were to my cheek and my nose, my chin, into my mouth. It was very late. We pulled ourselves together and she left for home from the cemetery. I wandered up to my mother's house, let myself in, dropped my clothes on the floor, and lay down on my bed.

In the still-dark morning my mother came in to wake me for chores. She woke me by rapping on my skull with her knuckles, a habit of hers I could never talk her out of. It seemed as if my head had just hit the pillow, and when I looked at the clock I could see that to be just about a fact.

"Where have you been?" she whispered, hissing the words urgently, fearfully. "Someone was in the cemetery. There were voices."

"It was me," I said. "I went to the fair with Afton and then we made love in the cemetery."

"You did no such thing," she said. "How can you talk like that?"

"It's the truth," I said.

"Only if it's true," she said. "You did no such thing."

"I have to sleep."

But instead of going, she sat down on the edge of my bed, her back rounded, her hands in her lap. She was worried about something else and I was grateful it wasn't me. She did not look at me, did not touch me, but kept her gaze steady, and her voice to me was clear and strong.

"Your father," she said. "He did not come home last night. I want you to go find him.

Silo

I WENT UP the road to the turnoff where I'd seen my father's car parked at the edge of the woods. It was a black Impala. He always bought black cars except for one time when he bought a blue car, a Biscayne, and swore he'd never do it again. He didn't give a reason why.

The morning was chill, and I had that rock in my gut from too little sleep, too much unspoken discussion with Afton, my head tired, my chest all glassy and brittle. My T-shirt dampened in the gray mists of a false dawn. The tar was dappled, and in the forest I could hear the ticking sound of leaves dripping, shedding the night, and all around me, the low undersound of the morning preparing for the cast of day's light.

I could see his car pulled off and the line it made told me it was the act of a man not in control. There was too much angle and it was too close to the run-out of a culvert, and a branch had swept the windshield.

I waded through the ferns and took their water, feeling it soak through my clothes, cold and hard, and only a few steps off the road I drew mosquitoes to my warm skin. I swatted at them and smacked them dead, bursting my own blood to flowers on my flesh. I cussed at them, swiping at the little snarls of blood they left, and thought, I ought not to have to do this. I was eighteen. I should be adventuring, my brain luxuriating in the workings of itself. My life should be the way I wanted it to be. I should not be up so early walking through these wet ferns looking for my father to bring him home.

When I pulled open the door, it was clear to me he had thrown up his liquor, clear to me by the way my eyes watered at the smell and my stomach went violent and I had to think strong thoughts to keep it somewhere south of my rib cage.

It was that lurch in my belly that grew me up some, made me a little older. That lurch, then and there, made me not so proud and distant, made me as weak as he was, made me realize all life can come to this. It's like taking out someone else's trash, or changing a diaper, or working the emergency room, or helping an old man settle onto the toilet, or collecting up the halves of your dead bird dog, cut in two by a train.

In your life you do these things, and they are what make you grow up. It's doing the things you wouldn't want to do if you had your druthers, and it's doing them in a time when the rest of the world doesn't care if they get done or not. It's doing them in an undramatic, undisciplined, unrequited way. It's doing them when you hate doing them and risk bitterness every step of the way. It was this simple: he was my father, and my mother had sent me off to find him, an errand that boys have been sent on for all time.

I leaned into the car and took him by his shoulder. I shook him and he flailed at me, wiped at his mouth, and groaned. He growled and told me to leave him alone. "Leave me alone," he said like a child, like someone hurt and ashamed. Then his stomach roiled again, but there was nothing left to come up and he only groaned.

"You have to go home," I told him. "She's worried about you."

"You leave me alone," he said.

"She's looking for you."

He'd come to by now and was trying to sit up but kept sliding down the seat. He took deep breaths through his nose and wiped at the front of his shirt. His bow tie dangled from his collar by a clip, and he knocked it loose with his wiping, sending it to the floor. It was clear to see that being awake and being sober brought him much pain.

"It's morning," I said. "You have to get cleaned up for work.

And that's when he took the time and told me in so many words he'd lost his job, a job he'd had since before I was born. It was a hard thing to imagine. He'd lost his job, and I could not picture him doing anything else. The factory was his life. I knew everyone there by their first names, not because I'd met them all but because he always talked about them, used to tell me funny things they'd said or done, told me about their lives, what they ate for lunch. All he knew was them and that job, and at the time he was as old as I am right now and to him it must have been like his family had asked him to leave and not come back, not even for a visit.

I went around to his side of the car and made him push over. I got in and backed onto the road. He lifted his knee to cross his legs and sat quietly as I made the short drive to the house. I wanted to be more, to do more, but I didn't. I parked in the driveway and shut off the engine. I got out and tossed the keys onto the front steps, made myself not look to the windows for fear of seeing my mother's face. Then I could not help myself and did look and she was there at the screen. I told her he had lost his job and she whispered she knew, so I turned away and crossed the lawn through the wet grass and jumped the fence into the pasture and began the half-mile walk to the farm.

I cut across lots, staying off the road, and picked up the shitty trail of the cows headed to the barn and then, in the fog down in the hollow, could see their swaying asses. I caught up and followed along, letting them set the pace, slow and meandering.

You didn't switch up the cows, didn't hurry them to their milking. It wasn't done, and it was the one time you slowed down and went along so easily you could fall asleep on your feet.

I could say I hated my father and at the same time felt sorry for him and felt sorry for myself, and while I was at it I could say I felt sorry for the whole fucking world, then hate myself for being so generous with sorriness and hatred. I could say that and I'd be right. I'd be on my heart's target.

I remembered how in the winter, before I left for Oswego to see Afton, my father and I had driven down to Massachusetts so I could be interviewed for a prep school. There was a man there who spoke to me about what kind of a person I thought I was, and then he spoke to the both of us and then to my father alone, about financial aid, of which we would need not a little.

When my father came out, his face was bathed in sweat and his hands were shaking. I could tell he needed a drink. The man looked at me and I took it to be a kind and understanding look, but I was torn between apologizing and wanting to burn down that school. I got my father into the car and found his pint for him in the trunk, under the spare tire, and drove him home. In a few weeks I'd be headed back there to start football practice. It seemed like years away, seemed imminent, too.

The cows before me, ambulant and rocking, swished and swatted. They coughed and belched. They stopped to browse. They separated and formed up again, the prospect of sweet grain on their minds.

I have thought a lot about a cow's mind, about what lies behind those huge, dark, liquid eyes, and have decided from time to time that their minds are like honey, viscous and sweet, and black like molasses. Theirs is a mind that finds itself in a body come to be a milk-producing machine. In 1872, a cow making six thousand pounds of milk in a year was considered an exceptional cow, and a hundred years later the mark of an exceptional cow became fifty thousand pounds of milk in a year.

Did those cows in front of me that morning and all the other mornings, did they sense the genetic tweaks made in their bodies, made to turn them fully lactational?

Halfway to the barn, my uncle pulled over in his pickup and let out Henry and Robb, his two best hired men, best in that they got up in the morning and worked hard and only Henry complained. They climbed the fence and waded the lush, wet grass and picked up some strays and dawdlers, said, "Come on girl, come on now," and gently directed them down to the path.

We said our "Morning"s, called each other by name, ant they fell in alongside me, trailing the cows to the barn. Henry and Robb were brothers and they worked every day of the year, with time off on Sunday afternoon, which meant they worked harder on Saturday to prepare for it.

We wandered along, our hips rocking, and we stopped to pluck stems of grass to chew. We did not speak to one another and often walked with a hand on the back of a straggler. It is true that people who tend animals come to be more like them, and it never does go the other way around. When tending cows, you don't hurry them, don't make sudden moves, don't speak but make sounds and whistles.

As we moved out of the hollow, the lights of the barn appeared on the horizon along with another set of lights, spots that made a bay of light up the stave silo. There was the boom of a crane rising to the sky, and a sound was coming now, the knocking sound of a big diesel engine.

The cows held up and began to bump into one another, to spread out from the path a hundred yards from the open gate and fill the field. We pushed them along, but they'd only go forward to mill and then veer off, as if the sound were a wall they couldn't pass through. Driving those cows was like raking sand. Henry and Robb got behind them again and held them, and I went on to the gate.

In the light I could see my uncle and my grandfather having a terrible argument at the wide-open barn door, hands flashing and arms waving. The old man had a way of bending his knees, ducking like a rooster and rising back up, when making his finer points. He walked off and everything went dark and the sound of the diesel died and I was left between the barn and the cows.

I could hear my uncle calling to me to bring on the cows. He said my name, said, "Come on, come on," not impatient but like it was okay now, it was safe to come ahead.

My uncle, my mother's brother, was my godfather, and I knew he must've talked to my mother and found out my father had lost his job. My mother and her brother were very close and spoke to each other three or four times a day. My mother was the oldest child and her sister was the second and then came my uncle. I was sure he knew my father hadn't come home that night. I was sure because he and my mother talked and because the argument he had with his father did not spill over onto me or Henry or Robb or anybody else that morning, did not spill over, because he was feeling bad for his sister.

Midmorning, after the milking, they started up the crane again. My uncle was now in a foul mood because all the commotion had upset the cows and dropped the milk down several hundred pounds. It'd been that way all week, he told me, wanted this business of the aerial photograph over and done with. He needed the cows to be as calm as possible, as set in their ways as method, so that he could read them for all their subtleties.

Everything told at the fair as to the ways of cows he already knew in his little finger, and these cows, the two hundred, you could point to any one of them and he could discourse on her production and predicated production, her genetic design and his intent in making up that design and his breeding of that cow to make it continue to be so. He could talk on her generations of mothers and fathers and how he made them to be what they were, and he could tell you of her offspring by number and gender.

Then again, he wasn't prone to discourse or even to talk much, as far as that goes. Maybe it was because his own father talked so much or maybe it was that he never talked much where I could hear him. So when the milking was done he left for his own farm in Walpole, where we ran heifers and raised corn and hay, and he stayed there the rest of the day. Because he'd left for the day, the old man took off, too, just to show that he also could do whatever he wanted.

He said, "He thinks he can just walk away. Well, I'll show him I can, too," and for that we were all grateful.

After breakfast I went to the wrecked truck and found Charley Dickard still asleep, wrapped up in feed bags and stretched across the seat. The inside of this vehicle didn't smell too damn sweet, and what I'd done in hiring him was now coming down on my shoulders. I'd hired him and now I'd have to work him.

"How you doing, Charley?" I said. "Ready to earn your keep?"

"I have felt worser," he said.

He sat up and looked around. The truck was junked under trees on the edge of the land, a place closed in and hidden from view. The truck was the most recent discard among rotting and rusting manure spreaders, broken-down running gears, feed wagons, and parts and pieces to who knew what.

I looked up to see if there was much sky above me, worried of a sudden for the old man's aerial photograph, and was relieved to see there was enough canopy so that this junkyard would not corrupt the picture. I was caught by how my worry for the picture betrayed me over to him. I whispered, "Fuck his photograph," just to make myself feel better.

Charley Dickard lay back down and sat up two or three times, and at first I thought there was system and intention behind his actions, something rigorous he did on first waking, like sit-ups or deep breathing. I thought about how long a goddamn day this was going to be. He moved as if he didn't know where he'd come to or how he'd got there. Finally he seemed to have his inner self balanced, his organs settled.

"You okay there? You going to make it?" I asked, handing over a sack of fried-egg sandwiches and a jar of coffee my grandmother had made up for him.

He studied the wrapping on one of the sandwiches and then neatly unfolded the wax paper in the exact reverse of how I'd seen her fold it. Then he lifted the bread and asked me if I had any catsup.

I told him no, I didn't have any on me at the time, and his response was more like he was just checking if I did, not that he really wanted it. It wasn't like it had anything to do with his sandwich, and by way of conversation I told him I preferred mustard on my fried-egg sandwiches, and he said mustard was good, too. Then it seemed okay to eat and he went about it in a most meticulous way, a cross between the high-born and a small wild animal, vulpine and artful.

I'd woken up crazy people before, watched them eat. I'd woken up crazy myself from this dream or that dream. I wondered how the full-blown crazy came from sleep to life. Was there a moment of lucidity, of peace, of knowing, and then terror and resolve that what they were would descend upon them in minutes, maybe seconds? As to the afflicted coming to wake, perhaps their sleep is crazed, too. Perhaps it resembles nothing like the sleep of the unafflicted, and so the to and fro gives no rest.

This to say, there is no rest for the afflicted. Like my father. When he was still allowed his drink in the house, I'd hear him in the dark morning get out of bed and walk to the kitchen past my door. I'd hear the refrigerator door open, and the snap and peel and hiss of a sixteen-ounce beer can, and a moment of silence. I'd hear half the can go down in a single draft and then a sigh, but he'd save the second half for when he shaved. Then the walks started coming in the middle of every night, and like when I woke him this morning, his lips would be checked and caked white and his mouth all cottony, so he couldn't speak but sounded like he was coming through snow or a pillow or from way, way off. How was it with his awakenings?

That morning I wished I had a cold one for him to drink, and then another and another and another, because that was what he wanted and needed.

"Charley," I said. "Charley Dickard. You going to make it? You got enough sleep for two men."

"I just have to undiscombobulate myself. I'm not normal, you know."

"In what way do you mean that?"

"Well, if I have to explain it to you, you'll never understand."

"That's good. You do just what you need to."

"I haven't slept in days. I couldn't sleep in jail. It's something I've never been able to do."

"I hear you," I said, and then egg and bread started falling out of his mouth and, surprised by its appearance, he'd stuff it back in, which made me feel a little better.

After he ate, I got him onto the painting. He listened intently, took instruction well, and I had confidence in him. It was simple work to paint the outside window casings, all of which could be reached by standing on a five-gallon bucket. It was my notion to slide off and watch that silo come down. I had no idea how they'd do it. Could they drag it down, maybe undermine it at the base and tip it over, timber it like a great tree? They had to be careful, as its foundation sat right next to the barn, near the intersection of the cross, and a false move would crash it onto and through the roof. After my morning, I wanted demolition.

I helped Charlie through several of the casings, and when he had it down I told him I had to run an errand and slid off to behind the barn to watch the demolition of the silo, a tall white-gray column of cement staves bounded with steel hoops, something like a lighthouse. Up there, like on Eye Hill, you could be the highest of anywhere around and see for miles, see Holsteins grazing the burnt-up pastures, see the seeps of water by the velvet green swales, a dog on a porch, the speck of equipment moving along a road, a man kneeling to weed, birch trees in the distance, white as egg.

We filled that silo every fall, and then all through the winter someone climbed up and in and began forking out ensilage to feed the cows. The last few years it'd become old and unsafe and didn't have enough capacity to bother with, so we made our silage in great bunkers dozed into the earth, and later in a bunker built on top of the earth with cement walls.

They had a silo at the county farm, too, a guarded silo because late in the year when the ensilage got low there were some feet of liquid corn squeezings in the bottom and they'd found prisoners in there, drunk and afloat.

I watched the men go up in a bucket, rising on the cable into the sky, and it was something I wanted to be doing. I liked these men. They were hard and wore T-shirts and jeans and steel hats, and they didn't seem burdened or smell like cow shit. They wore gloves and sunglasses and moved quickly, and when they did something it was done and they wouldn't be doing it again and again every day of every year. They laughed and made smart-ass remarks, yelled back and forth in a friendly way. They had tools and mechanisms I did not know the workings of. I liked the way they carried their cigarettes rolled up in one sleeve of their T-shirts and lit cigarettes off hot objects like the exhaust pipe or a cutting torch, the way they smoked those cigarettes, like they were smoking their hand or something very fine.

I knew how to grow and produce while they knew how to build and destroy; I knew animal and plant and these men knew rock and mineral.

I watched them go up the line with a fifteen-pound sledge hammer, then knock holes in under the steel dome roof at four points, equidistant the way around, working from the bucket and I saw where they used hand signals to tell the operator what to do. I stood close to watch him feather the sticks with his fingers to make the cable, boom, and jib do what the men in the bucket wanted done. Each cable and hook and maneuver was of a kind and had a name, and they spoke in their own language, spoke those names while I listened to them, hanging around where they were on the pretense of the old man's telling me I was supposed to be there in case they needed any help.

After knocking in the holes, they went back up and set cables, and then a single man rode the hook up to the top of the silo, one foot on the crook and the other on the point. From up high he directed the operator to raise the boom, to cable down, to cable up, to snug the cables. He made the hook-up and stood on the ball at the junction of force and resistance.

The engine powered up and the crane shuttered under load and then, as easy as lifting a dish, the dome eased into the air and hung there, swaying in the wind like a moon they had captured. The operator swung the boom and lowered the dome and its size increased as it loomed to earth.

The men stopped work to take a break, to open their lunch buckets. I went back around the barn to check on Charley. He was down on his knees, his face about hovering in a paint can, sucking paint fumes to the inside of his skull.

"Jesus Christ, Charley, you can't be doing that," I said. Charley Dickard looked up and started right in with his crazy talk, jabbering and yammering away. I calmed him down and told him that what windows he'd done he'd done fine, a real fine job.

"I know," he said. "It's just that I get the most violent headaches with the stuff."

I told him to keep working and I'd bring him some lunch.

In the house the old man was sitting in his place. He told me he'd seen my hired man with his face in the paint bucket but did not want to disturb him, and he assumed I'd taken care of it. He wanted to know if the painting would be done and I told him I did take care of it and he said to go ahead and eat my pork chops.

About then my mother came bustling in. She went straight to the kitchen and I could hear her and my grandmother getting into it. Then she came into the dining room and confronted her father and asked why she hadn't been told about the cancer.

I could see what was coming. It was like the moment before a bar fight breaks out. The air gets quiet and then it begins to swell and you have to make a quick decision as to whether this one is your concern or not, because it's all about to happen. If it isn't your concern, you get low and head for the corners. If it is, your ambition is to get in the first lick or two and then grab on and hold and ride it, and by all means, do not lose your feet. I made my decision and got my head so close to that pork chop on my plate I could lick it.

The old man grunted. My mother was one of the few people on earth who could tell him his business, and only because she rarely did. In turn, he rarely listened. She started in with her chewing-tobacco theory, pestering my grandmother with it, because my grandmother had recently bought him a brass spittoon.

"It's not for him to use, young lady. He is forbidden to use it," my grandmother said.

I could vouch for that. It was only for show she bought it. She wouldn't let you spit in it. She made you use a Maxwell House coffee can.

"Well, what about him?" he said, pointing at me. "He chews. Get after him about it."

She shot me a look that said I was as bad as could be and went back after him. He grunted some more and she told him he'd better face up to this and he told her that the way he saw it she'd better be taking care of her own family and doing it up the road. She went red in the face, gave a look between terror and pain, and started to cry. He told her to leave his house if she was going to cry, so she left. And I made myself even smaller because of the hate I felt for him. He had no right to tell her that, had no right to speak to her that way, and I was ashamed because other times I had done it, too.

We went back to eating and I mentioned to my grandmother that, if it was okay, I'd like to take a plate of food out to Charley Dickard. She told me to go ahead. I heaped up a plate with pork chops and mashed potatoes and green beans and applesauce and bread and took it out to him. He was sitting on the five-gallon bucket, his arms folded and his legs crossed, staring off into the beyond or maybe at something as near as the black darters that floated past in the fluid of his eyeball. He did the same staring thing with the food, asked me about catsup and all that.

"Are you asking because you want catsup?" I asked him.

"Well, what do you think?" he said, like I was the one supposed to be crazy.

Back in the house the old man was on the phone. He was talking to my mother.

He was saying, "I don't want any minister up here on Sunday. Sunday should be a day of rest, especially for a goddamn minister . . . I don't know if I've been baptized. I don't want anybody here for Sunday . . . I want everybody to be gone. I'm having my aerial photograph taken on Sunday . . . Have the minister to your own house."

She could be unremitting when she got something in her head. She held to the eternal, the constant, and the incessant. All life was for everlasting, perpetual and interminable down to its smallest parts. To like a food was to like it forever. To decide on a person was to hold that opinion to the grave.

I sometimes try to think what of me is her and what of me is my father. I think I hold within me the essence of both of them, the essence of their strengths and weaknesses, but that's as far as I ever get, just something vague like the nature of the wind. Maybe what we hold within us of our parents is only something like the weather, their weather passed into us. It can be changeable, stormy to placid, serene, then violent, or always of a single kind, like the desert or the tundra. Weather has what is human insofar as it can be strong and eternal or weak and desirous in how it touches, and its caress can elevate, can destroy.

My grandmother sat in the eye of this storm drinking her tea, whispering for him not to talk that way to her, and then smiling at me, asking me if I'd had enough to eat, asking me if I thought it was as lovely a day as she did. I told her yes, it was a beautiful day outside, and she said, "Good, good," and mentioned her asparagus and rhubarb and how ripe her tomatoes were. My grandmother was a lady from a different time and a different place. She was civil and wanted for there to be harmony. She liked the peaceful side of beauty.

I left the house and got Charley back to work and went around to the silo. The men were up in the bucket again, working their way around, knocking the silo staves into the center of the column. They worked their way down and it took time, so I found a cool place in the shade where I could be on call in case they needed help, which of course they wouldn't.

When I woke up, they had the knocking-in part of the job done and the silo was a pile of cracked cement and rotten silage. From around the barn I could see Afton coming by on her bicycle and could feel myself falling into the love I was in all over again, and, as quickly, my mind went to my father and I tried to remember when that'd been, that morning walk through the ferns to the side of his car. Should I say to her it was this morning, or earlier, or yesterday? Should I even tell her?

"You better come here," she was saying. "You better take a look at this."

I followed her around and could see black paint splattered everywhere, with Charley swinging a bucket over his head.

"You put that down," I told him. Whether he stopped the bucket in arc for long enough or whether centrifugal force is a law of nature that crazy people cannot depend on, the paint poured from the bucket and drenched Charley's head and shoulders and down to his shoes. It was amazing to watch.

I was able to get a hose onto him and the wall and wash away all but a shadow of black on both, and my grandmother had some clothes of the old man's that were set aside for the Salvation Army, which she let me have. After he wandered away for the night, Afton stood around during chores and talked with my uncle while he stripped out cows and I fed out the grain, and afterwards she came into the house and had a grilled-cheese sandwich and a bowl of tomato soup. She chatted with my grandmother, who smiled at her, and then she called to tell her grandmother where she was and how I'd give her a ride home.

Then me and Afton sat on the porch eating vanilla ice cream, listening to a moth go crazy on the light bulb, listening to the Red Sox game on the radio. We did the shadow of things, lived in the small, poised moments like this, listened to but a few innings on the radio. It was here where life could be paused over and held and wondered on. It was a plotless life insofar as it lacked all but the most profound beginnings and endings. Life and work were the same and were unchanging.

Me and Afton wondered about this place and that place and about memory and how it worked, its intricacies, its dependability. She had moved thirteen times as a child and remembered something of every place she lived. Moving so much, she told me, had made her depend on herself, made her have a place inside she could go to to find peace and quiet, and I had not moved at all and was still the same way as she was about a place inside. We came to agree that moving was okay, but too much or too little was a bad thing.

I asked her how she thought it was with crazy people when they woke up, and her thoughts on the subject were that maybe they did have a moment of sanity and then felt themselves to be sliding to madness again. She said she was feeling a little blue, fearing the dreams she'd been having, dreams about a baby inside her and the doctor telling her how this was a baby she wanted to have. I went very quiet and my thoughts dwelled on Afton's baby dream and what it could mean, and I was and wasn't afraid.

The old man pulled in about then from some adventure of buying and selling cows. He was in good spirits, so I assumed that he'd made out all right, assumed that maybe twenty or thirty cows had swapped hands, twenty thousand dollars' worth of livestock, or maybe only a hundred dollars' in calves, but that anyhow he'd made money.

He sat right down with us and was gentle and polite, asked Afton question after question about her and her family, and she answered each one. Then a sadness came over him as he no doubt remembered what all resided in his body. I asked him if he was okay, if I could get him something.

He said, "I guess I got the hiccups now and I can't get rid of them." I knew what he meant but I went for a glass of water anyway. When I came out he was cheery again and he and Afton were in the midst of something funny.

The next summer I would hire on to work construction with the company that took down the silo. My summer after prep school and before college would be spent coming up out of the ground on a crest of concrete and steel in White River Junction, Vermont. In single mornings, we'd pour a hundred and fifty yards of concrete, and I learned things like a cubic foot of concrete weighs a hundred pounds and there are twenty-seven cubic feet in a cubic yard. The superintendent would be singing out, Never let the setting sun see a day that some concrete doesn't run, and like farm work, it was work that could hurt you.

I rode to work with a man called the Russian. He'd been in the navy too young, and when his mother pleaded for his discharge they found him on a ship in the North Sea, guarding the brig and wearing some fine new tattoos.

How true the story I don't know, because I've heard versions of it from every war.

I learned to tie steel from a hard-boiled iron worker named Blackie, who drank a six-pack every day for lunch. Later in the summer, a guy named Vern hired on. He'd been a stick man on a survey crew for the Alaska pipeline and was waiting for Congress to approve the construction. He told stories of polar bears and exploding helicopters and wages beyond belief. He had a one-way ticket in a locker in Boston, and the day the permits came through, he'd be gone. He said I could come, too, and for a time I anguished over the decision I made not to chuck it all and head off to Alaska. I was headed for college instead.

Working the construction job, I would learn another way of story, story as passing on the burden of danger. As story was told around the campfire to keep awake, to keep back the night, story was told to me here to say, Best keep awake, keep alert or your ass could be grass and mine, too. You could hold those stories until a new guy showed up, and you passed them on to him to see if he would flinch. You wanted to know because some people had a kind of luck it was important to avoid.

Another moth flew in to assault the light bulb. The old man smoked his cigar and touched his temple, tapped his cane. Charley Dickard came strolling over in his new clothes. Cy and Lila had agreed to take him in, he said, as long as he didn't give Lila any shit—otherwise she'd stick a knife in him, said those very words—and that seemed agreeable to him. The old man looked at him and couldn't help but smile.

"Where the hell did that getup come from?" he said.

"Why, Paris fucking France. Where do you think?" Charley told him, and we all laughed. Then the old man went to talking about trees he'd plant that'd take years to grow to maturity and how late in the fall he'd contour the land on the lower meadow to reduce the flooding, contour the land to conserve the soil.

In the few years before he died, I'd come home to visit and be struck by how he wasn't as big as I remembered him, really couldn't walk on water. A last picture I have of him is in a souvenir program for the Cheshire County Fair. It is in memoriam because he had passed away that Easter. It tells that he was born June 26, 1907, and was the fifth generation to own and farm the home place and that he was well known in the oxen and cattle field and was a great supporter of the fair and seldom missed the pulling events.

In the picture he still had the look in his eye. The look was narrow and intense, and at the same time the self-delight was apparent. It's a look that says, The past is the past, but what about right now? What are we going to do now that will make a past worth remembering? And, too, there was the cold mortal eye of cancer that I could see because of what I knew.

"Hey, Charley," the old man said, taking off his fedora. "Catch."

Charley caught the fedora and scrutinized it. He stroked the crease and brushed it with the back of his sleeve. Then he set it on his head, gave the brim a tug, and flashed his lunatic smile. The old man thought that was pretty special, told him that now, for sure, he looked like Paris fucking France, right from the box.

A Day Like Platinum

FRIDAY BROKE OUT, a day like platinum, and it was hard to imagine in all that light that there was something as bad as dying or to even say that dying was a bad thing. On the farm it was hard to imagine the body's having wants except for sleep. You worked very hard and were affirmed in that work: what you planted grew and fed the stock, which, in turn, fed you. There was milk to drink, more milk made in a single day than a body could ever drink in a lifetime, and beef and vegetables, and as long as there was diesel in the thousand-gallon tanks there would be fuel to run the generator for lights and power. The farm was its own world and it was where I was from, not this town or state or region or country but here, the farm.

It was days breaking like this that made the work seem worth it, that gave rise to such ponderings, and it is how fixed these thoughts are in my brain, how fixed the farm is in its place outside the world, that has always made me think I can go home. I can actually be there in a few hours because it is not just a place of the mind but a place itself. It is real. It is land to be walked, land to be owned as long as there is the rule of law. Even if the law were to fail, I know it is land that people would die for.

And on that platinum day, at first break of light, Afton showed up to work, to help with the painting. The old man had asked her the night before if she wanted to work a few days. She didn't tell me, because she wanted to surprise me.

I told her I was glad she was here but I didn't like surprises. I told her I didn't like presents either, as far as that went. I didn't mean to say it; it just came out.

She told me she was sorry by saying, "I like you in your cowboy pants."

"These," I said, looking down at myself. By chance I was wearing a pair of brown canvas pants, ones I usually kept for winter.

"Here," she said. "I made you some oatmeal cookies."

"Oh," I said. "I like oatmeal cookies."

"No, you don't. I can tell."

"How can you tell?" I asked, but she wouldn't answer me and started painting while I went over to Lila's to sneak some doughnuts and rouse Charley. He was already on the hoof and met me halfway. He was wearing the old man's fedora and seemed quite proud to be under that hat. I told him he looked mighty dapper and we all went to painting the window frames. Later on we topped off the last heaping truckload of junk and rubbish to head for the gully.

And, too, on that platinum day, the word was out about the old man's cancer, and so came the parade of Lincolns and Cadillacs and New Yorkers and Buicks. The old man's brothers and sisters were coming to see him. We didn't mark time with birthdays and holidays and vacations, didn't come together for such events. Instead, we marked it with birth and death, and this death was going to be one of the greatest of all time, the death of greatness itself, the beginning of death in their own generation.

Eight years ago they buried their mother, my great-grandmother. She was ninety years old and had borne a generation of titans, eleven of them in all.

His brothers and sisters, they hummphed and hrrred, spoke old-people language about lungs and hearts and colons and veins and kidneys and blood and fluids. They knew of cancers and strokes and diabetes. Some brought their must-have medication, and one brought her oxygen bottle, which I helped her in with. The brothers and sisters also knew how to make money and had done so in railroads and cattle and land and fuel oil and banking and insurance. They were born into the beginning of the century, when king dogs were divvying up the globe's land and water, and steel was replacing iron.

His brothers didn't stay in the house for long. They walked around the barns, where they were more comfortable, and I knew their minds. They were wondering if my uncle would be able to make a go of it. They were making tallies and calculating the worth of the land, the rolling stock, the cows, sizing up the place as if preparing an offer to buy, but it was not out of any greed or callousness. It was their most natural activity to make this deal or that deal, and because there were so many of them they were often after the same deal, whether it was in Ontario or Florida, and took much delight in putting the screws to one another.

The old man's sisters stayed inside and pestered him, and I knew he liked their attention. They were grand women who didn't give a shit about the small things in life, the small and petty concerns. The greatness of those ladies is confirmed in my head, their closeness to one another, their love of horse racing and the stock market, their many children and the way they dispensed their opinions, their wit, their largess without a care. They were nosey with a passion and none of them—none of the brothers either—seemed to know limitation. Their interiors were their business.

"I hear you're getting ready to have your picture taken," one of the brothers said to me.

"How you doing, Charley?" he yelled to Charley Dickard.

Charley came over and told how good he was doing, and the old man's brother gave him a cigar, complimented him on his wearing of the old man's hat.

"You going to be around long?"

"Long as I'm needed," Charley said.

"Good, good," my great-uncle said, lighting Charley's cigar and one for himself and rolling it in his lips to wet the end and Charley doing exactly the same thing.

"Charley, where'd you get those clothes?

"Paris fucking France. Where do you think?"

"Good. Good."

On their way to leave, the brothers and sisters each said how big a boy I was and asked if Afton was my girl-friend and palmed me a ten or a twenty. Then they drove off like big, slow birds, to light again in their houses in Boston and Keene and Walpole or maybe Maine or Flor-ida. One great-uncle, near to seventy years old, hard of hearing, started his car but could not hear it started and so ground the ignition until I told him it was running. Then he backed away into a tractor and looked over his shoul-der, over his cigar, all pissed off as if the tractor had hit him. He got himself into forward and headed down the road and almost struck a car coming his way. Both drivers oversteered and swiped into the bushes, ground their tires in the gravel on the berm.

The car coming his way pulled in and stopped. If he was angry, I didn't want any part of it, so I headed for the truck where Afton was waiting. I was getting in the truck when the minister stepped out of his car. He'd come by that day of his own accord. In his white sneakers with white socks and white shorts and a short-sleeve white shirt, he was a minister in disguise, but he carried a small-sized Bible.

I was suspicious of him without reason. It was just the way he had learned to listen, his furrowed brow and the tilt of his head, the way he'd nod his head on the stem of his neck, not so much in concert with what was being said but clocklike, nodding rapidly at timed intervals. Some people are born listeners, some listen out of politeness or interest or eagerness, but he was like someone who'd learned to listen, and his nodding head was like a pump drawing information out of me. His looking I feared, looking that went right into my still-black soul when he should have been listening.

So when he said, "How have you been?" and "I haven't seen you in a while," and this and that about the state of the church and the activities of the various youth groups, it was I who felt like the terminal man he'd come to see, like it was I he intended to baptize and save before the end, so to send me on my way in the name of Jesus Christ himself.

He asked if my grandfather was around. He wanted to meet him. I said he was and he was in a terrible way and I did not think he wanted to talk to him or to anybody else.

"Well, why don't we let him decide," he said, all sweetlike.

I don't know why—call it an inspired moment—but I pointed to Charley Dickard, sitting on the five-gallon bucket smoking his cigar, and I said, "Well he's right there, if you insist, but he doesn't want to talk. He's hostile right now. His mind isn't right, but you go ahead."

The minister thanked me and shook my hand and I told him, "Yeah, anytime," and he started towards Charley.

Charley saw him coming and stood and started wandering off. The minister looked back at me and I shrugged and nodded, meaning, Go ahead, go ahead, and so he did and Charley Dickard kept distance between them. The minister walked on and Charley kept going and the minister followed him, calling out my grandfather's name, and I didn't know it then, but that'd be the last I'd see of the both of them for a long, long time to come. This event would become known as *that little stunt I pulled on the minister.*

I turned the ignition and the truck roared to life. Its muffler had long since rusted away, and the sound coming from underneath took a great throaty chunk out of the air, ate up the sounds of the farm. But it was not enough to make me forget that I had just done something for which there might be hell to pay. What I should have done was engage him, have a discussion, maybe ask him about all those Catholics and Jews getting into heaven, and the dogs and the cats and the cows and squirrels, or was it to be only sheep? I threw the truck in gear and we pulled onto the tar road. Down the hill we took up the dirt road to the river, jouncing along as merry as we could be.

I drove slowly down that road, took my time. Now that the word was out, it'd be easy to disappear, to be lazy for a while and not be missed. There'd be more relatives and friends and neighbors come by to torment the old man with their concern.

Afton, dusty and flecked with paint, was beside me on the hard bench seat, and her skin showed red from the sun. She had a blister on her hand, and her palms and fingers ached. I was at loose ends, canceling this thought, emptying my brain of that one. I felt to find where the sun was on my neck, felt the trickle of sweat down my back. My own hands, hard and raw and cracked, were dulled to pain, and then, her hand was resting on my knee as if that were where it belonged.

We drove over a culvert and stopped to catch some newts in the wet ground to the left of it and let them run up our arms and necks. They were orange and spotted and dartlike in the shallows at the edges of the soggy pond, where the lily pads splayed, and any August day you could see their slim, wagging bodies skittering through the water, away from the parched, checkered ground. To the right, the land fell away into deepness, hemlocks rooted to the banks, and that was where the pipe came clear. Sometimes the water foamed from its mouth.

We drove on past the ground charred from the fire some nights ago, and already it was greening at the edges. In the passing I tried to think about our night out there, but my mind could not hold on for long. It was like trying to think about life itself, so I went to remembering the swelter from the fire that night, the queasy feel of sunstroke that came from being too close and unable to turn away. I could remember the elements of the fire, knelling and chiming and popping and whizzing and striking out. I could hear it eating away at itself, consuming what gave it life, and speculated, asked Afton, If it wasn't a flood again but fire, what would the ark become?

"Rocket ships? I don't know. Good question."

At the drop of land, I clutched and downshifted. It was a good habit not to trust the brakes on any of the older farm vehicles. We slowed and swung right, and I backed in as near to the edge of the gully as possible and shut down the engine. Then we both just sat, letting silence come back to us until we could hear our hearts in our chests, feel our blood in our ears.

We drank from a water jug I had, and kissed and drank and let water into each other's mouths, let it run down our chins and necks, and sighed and laughed until we ran out of water. It could have been a few minutes or a few hours, or even a few seasons could have winged by for all that I knew, but at some point I saw a stack of boxes and did not recognize them as junk of ours.

There were three boxes and they sat to the edge under a tree, more like they were waiting to be picked up than thrown away. I pointed them out to her and she became curious, too, so we got down from the truck and I took out my jackknife and cut one open.

Inside were books, fifty or sixty of them. They were all the same, with powder-blue covers, the edges of the pages made raggedy on purpose and sewn together with a silky thread. The title was *My Life*, and inside it said the books were published two years ago by Happiness Press. The poems seemed okay to me. They were sincere and full of dreams and wishes and regrets and confessions of failures.

We sat on the running board looking at the books while sparrows fluttered and swooped about us, birds bearing streamers of husk. A praying mantis stood in the long grass, depending on his iridescent body to hide him. The poems were about that, too, about seeing and thinking and birds in flight and industrious bees and gentle animals, and a lot about love, love of thee and thou.

I asked her who she thought thee and thou were and she told me probably a woman, like I had not enough brain to get that far.

"Really?" I said. "Do you really think so?" and she laughed and punched me in the arm. Then she read a poem or two aloud and of a sudden, when given a voice, they did not seem so good. Maybe it was because they were to a woman, and so for a woman to read them sounded funny.

You try, she said, and I did and they still did not sound right to our ears.

'"What should we do?" I said. "We can't just leave them here for the weather. Maybe he'll change his mind and come back. He'll realize they aren't too bad and come for them, like someone who leaves a child and then returns for it." I said all that and she gave off her sometimes-you're-strange look.

"One thing is clear. You shouldn't read any more of this stuff. It affects your brain."

I knew who the poet was. I told Afton it was the skier. These past winters, in the clipped days of nothing, I'd watch him skirting the lower meadow, a rifle strapped to his back. He conveyed himself over the stark white winter snow, across the glare of snow ice, corn snow, snow like grain, knee-deep powder, snow that had been bid by the wind, hilled and ridged and rippled like corduroy, snow glazed to be hard as glass.

He looked more like he was swimming than ski-ing. He was in training as a pentathlete. Some people said he was the fastest skier on the team but couldn't shoot straight. He had to learn to shoot between heart-beats, between breaths, so he came every day, that ri-fle strapped to his back, crossed silently, in and out of the snow blink, knowing he was faster than anyone but couldn't hit the target.

"Watching him is how I decided to come see you," I said, and she smiled. "Oh, well, what should we do?"

"We should leave them here in case he changes his mind."

"Maybe he wants them discovered, like some old-fuck

poet will happen along and think they are really great poems and make this guy famous in spite of himself."

"That's a nice thought, but this doesn't exactly look like
the kind of place where old-fuck poets wander."

"Where do they wander, then?"

"I don't know. How should I know?"

"I don't know," I said. "But if I were an old-fuck poet I'd
wander here."

"That's because you live here." Then her voice was soft
and quiet and she asked me if I thought I could get off
work on Sunday. We could take her grandmother's car
and drive somewhere, spend the day together. Without
thinking about how I'd ever do such a thing, I told her yes,
and she smiled.

I got up and stretched, felt strong in myself. I climbed
into the bed of the truck and got my weight against an old
refrigerator perched to the back. My plan was to wrestle
it forward, get it rocking, and then slide around behind
it and give it a heave to send it toppling over the edge.
It seemed like a good thing to do to keep from flying to
pieces over the thought of spending a day with Afton.

I got it moving, balanced to tip off its front corners,
and made another step when of a sudden I felt snake-
bit. I held poised and looked down and could see there
was a stub of two-by-four attached to my foot. Then I
felt the pain come again. The pain was out there somewhere, not really mine, and then it became mine in no
uncertain terms.

I pulled away, my foot still nailed to the wood, and lost
my balance. The refrigerator weighed me to the edge until

I was falling with it into the gully, falling down through the rusty cutter knives and busted-up mason jars, burned-out motors, and bent cowlings and sacks of rotten bale twine and grease buckets and crushed pails and medicine bottles and snapped harness, broken implements, and dead calves, their bones licked clean. I hit and tumbled, and at the swampy bottom I stopped myself by plunging my hand through the only unshattered pane of glass within a half mile, coming up with a slashed wrist.

I held up my hand and could see the red and, behind it, fuzzy in my vision, the splays of green lily pad and, nearer to me, pesky cockleburs and clusters of stinging nettles. I could see a lot of suns in the sky. I thought, I have ripped my pants. I have hurt myself.

I looked up and could see her way at the top, horror on her face. I waved to show her I was okay and she cried out because my wrist was cut so bad. It was bleeding pretty good and I could see down into the meat, but nothing spurting or pumping, just a whole lot of blood. My thinking was how relieved I was I got hurt because now I'd have an excuse not to work on Sunday, and then I went back to considering my pain.

The truck was not legal for the highway, but we took it anyway. It was a truck you had to have a personal relationship with if you were going to drive it, so I drove. My spiked left foot wasn't too bad because the clutch was soft, and by listening to the engine you could shift at speed without using it at all. Because it was my right wrist, she had to shift, and it all worked so well we could have driven around all day like that. I told her we had to write this up for *Reader's Digest,* one of those real-life adventures, and she did not think that was too funny.

I hobbled into the emergency room, wincing with each step, my foot bleeding wet and sticky inside my shoe. In the hospital I was most aware of how dirty I was, how much I smelled of the farm. Afton helped me along. She had bound my wrist with her white cotton underpants, and even in pain, I thought that was a terribly funny thing. She had to smile, too, but they were the cleanest thing we could find to stanch the blood.

The pain in my foot had gone to a throb by then, sharp at the edges and capable of sending messages. I felt dizzy and saw the floaters in my eyes, dark lunettes and spirals and gears and pieces of gears, all like parts from tiny watches. I needed to sit down but was afraid I'd get cow shit on the chair. Afton was beautiful to me and I told her so and she rolled her eyes. She looked like she wore sun dust, and around her eyes it made rays of lines.

About then my mother showed up. I don't know how she heard. She looked at me and said, "I hope you're satisfied now."

She hustled me over to the elevator, Afton following along, and I was sad for her because she did not know how to be. My mother got me up the floors to a doctor who was waiting for us, the doctor who had been my pediatrician. He'd sewn me up before, given me tetanus shots, and one time he took a bean out of my nose. He got me into a room and went to work on me, and it was not a pleasant experience. I could see down in my wrist the shards and flecks and dirt and matter that had to come out, could see the meat and bone and trails of blood, could see needles entering and the shiny stainless steel clutching and plucking and sliding. I heard him say how lucky I was and asked him if he was going to put me out.

"I don't need to," he said. "Turn your head and look the other way."

"I can't help but look," I said, and he nodded like he understood and went back to work. After a while it was like it wasn't me being worked on, and I told him the old man had prostate cancer. He said he'd heard that.

Then he said a funny thing for a doctor, said, "When I die of cancer, I hope I'm on a motorcycle doing ninety and all the nurses have big tits." I know he said it because I wrote it down that night, and the handwriting is significant because I had to write it with my left hand.

When I came out, Afton and my mother were waiting for me. My mother drove us back to the farm, where Afton said maybe we should call off Sunday. I said no.

"Then I'll pick you up?"

"Yes," I said, and she got her bicycle and rode away.

"I hope you learned something," my mother said.

"Yes, I did," I told her. "When you are about to die, your whole life really does flash before your eyes."

The old man was even less sympathetic. It was his conviction that I hurt myself on purpose and he said as much and then he fired me again. But there was more to it than that. The minister had sent Charley Dickard over the edge and Charley was hiding in the woods somewhere, yelling cuss words from behind trees, upsetting the cows. The old man knew it was all my fault and was convinced Charley Dickard was going to burn down the place.

My mother went on to tell me again and again, "Your grandfather has the cancer and he may not have much time." She didn't want us to fight during our last chance to spend time together.

I told her I did not quit, I was fired. I wanted to tell her the old man and me would no doubt have a long time in hell together but held myself back on that one. It wasn't that I couldn't say that to her, it was just that she would have believed it for sure.

"Tomorrow," I said, "me and Afton are going away for the day."

"You go ahead," she said. "You do what you want to anyway."

Billy called later that night from somewhere on the road and told me they were at the Campground of Truth. They'd picked up some hitchhikers who were destined for the place and so drove them the whole way. It was in Ohio, he thought, although he could not seem to get a clear answer, because they'd tagged along the borders of Ohio and Pennsylvania for a ways. It was a commune of sorts and Tucker had decided this would be his first great adventure on the road. He'd taken up with a commune woman and there was talk of a mass marriage.

Billy said that Tucker was real happy and that he himself would hang out for a few more days and then hitch back. I told him when he got close to give me a call and I'd come get him.

This was the year the cancer decided on the old man and began its fatal caress. It was the year both my father and my grandfather began their dying, and neither could help themselves. There were accidents happening in their bodies and brains, silent collisions, wreckage that took place further back in time and only now was apparent.

When my mother heard the news about her father, her first thought was what God might say. He must have directed her to join the Cancer Society, because she did and began shaking down the neighbors for contributions as if she alone could raise the cash to fund the breakthrough to save his life. This was the year my father could not turn back, could not turn away from his drink, began his own sad descent toward death. But with him there was no news, no society, just anonymity. It'd been telling of itself already for years and years, and now it was just day by day.

Air

It was Sunday morning and I'd not be going back to work, back to the daylong and nightlong days. I'd fought with the old man in the past, but not like the night before. I didn't much care anyway. He claimed I had gotten hurt on purpose and, to his credit, had me believing such, had me believing that I had driven my foot down onto the spike and had leaped from the bed of the truck into the gully.

All through the night, Charley Dickard could be heard yelling threats against us and himself and the world from the woods, having moved there from up behind the barn and from the meadow and then from the corn. He'd say my name or the old man's name and then some garbled shit about damnation and eternity. I let my mind wander and imagined him there in the woods, chewing on some part of the now-dead minister and longing for some catsup. Sometime close to the morning light it was quiet, so he must have fallen asleep.

I moved in and out of sleep that night as the pain and his voice from the forest would let me. When I was awake, I'd hear him saying, "You were going to shoot me, you were going to shoot me . . . I know people, I know people." When I slept, I was falling again and again into that gully, down into junk and refuse and garbage, Charley yelling from the hollow: "Let me tell you about Jesus fucking Christ, the Lord our Savior. Believe in the Lord and have eternal fucking life!"

After one such vivid descent, I got out of my bed for a glass of water. I could see my mother sitting outside in a chair. She was wrapped in a blanket, and the lawn was pearly white with dew and the moon was so big and close it looked like it was waiting to be touched. My mother was staring off into the woods in the direction of the farm across the hollow, in the direction the sounds of Charley Dickard were coming from.

I went out and sat down in the wet grass next to her chair. I wanted to tell her to come inside, tell her it was nothing to worry about and everything would be okay, but my mother was not the kind of person to be patient with only soothing talk. She knew everything would not be okay. She knew the world was taking on a change. In a few years she would no longer be a daughter.

Then she whispered, "He's a rotten devil, that Charley Dickard."

I wanted to make up conversation. I wanted to tell her about the books I'd found at the edge of the gully, wanted to spin on about what all I wanted to do in life, wanted to confess to her that I wanted travel and adventure, wanted to be a writer, but she had begun to weep and sitting beside each other was as close as we came.

"Reject sin . . . Banish your fears . . . Believe in the Lord," we heard. Then, from across the hollow, the old man bellowed out from his upstairs bedroom window, "Fuck you, Charley Dickard. Fuck you. You just go fuck yourself."

"You tell him," she said. And then she was smiling, then laughing.

In the morning light I wandered my empty house, hobbled about. Everyone had gone off to church. It'd been a few months since I'd spent a morning in my mother and father's house. I walked the sunlit rooms, weighing the one foot and going light on the other. Being hurt was no big thing by now, just some pain and carefulness. The doctor told me I'd probably miss a few days of football practice but otherwise I'd be okay for the season.

I made a cup of instant and sat on the front steps, and after a while my father came walking down the road. He had started walking a lot some years before, when he lost his license for a time. It was a habit he got into and kept up after they returned it to him. Losing the license and the delirium tremors might just have impressed upon him how his life was going, and we held out for change. It was change that never came.

He turned into the driveway and from a distance he looked young and fit. He smiled and I smiled back and held up my cup to salute him.

"Watch this," he said and he hurdled over the back of the lawn chair my mother had been sitting in the night before. "Bet you can't do that," he said, and I told him no, I didn't think I could, at least not today, and we laughed.

He said, "Are you hungry?"

"Sure, I'll eat something."

We went inside and while the bacon cooked he sliced raw potatoes, poured the bacon grease into another skillet, and then cooked the potatoes. He had a way to make the outsides crisp, almost black, and I've never had potatoes that good in my whole life ever again. He cooked with a towel over his shoulder, and I thought he could get a job doing that. But it wasn't something I could actually see him doing.

He took up the pepper can and peppered the potatoes real good. He poured some ginger ale into a glass and went out to the garage, and when he came back the glass was full and he tended to the breakfast he was cooking for me and sipped at his drink.

"What are you doing today?" he asked.

"Me and Afton are driving up to Fort Ticonderoga."

"Remember when we went up there?"

"Yes," I said. "It was really nice."

"You got enough money? You all set?"

I nodded. I was all set.

"I heard you got in a fight with your grandfather."

"Doesn't look good."

Then he told me a story about how, when he was first dating my mother, he drove out from Keene to show her a new car he'd bought. The old man got him to drive off into the up-country to see a man about a pair of oxen. It was a sloppy winter day, the back roads rutted and potted, and my father's new car took a beating as it tailed and sashayed over the hill roads. He said the old man had bargained hard for better than an hour and finally they left in a huff. At the foot of the ox owner's farm road—and by now it was dark and snowing—the old man told him to pull over and wait. The old man lit a cigar and after a few minutes the owner came driving down, looking for them to agree to the deal the old man wanted.

"It was the damndest thing I ever saw," my father said. "And to top it off, when we got back I found out he'd just bought a new car, too, but hadn't wanted to take it out in that weather."

My father laughed over the breakfast he was cooking. He thought it was the funniest thing, what the old man had done to him when he was my age. When the old man finally died, my father cried and went to his bed and got in under the covers and stayed there for three days, stayed sober in his grief.

As the potatoes were getting done, he turned up the heat on the bacon and moved the slices off to the edge. Then he cracked two eggs into the grease and you could hear them sizzle and snap in the pan, the whites coming on and the yolks shaking like jelly. Already my mouth was watering and my stomach was working up whatever chemicals it'd require for this particular feed. In the grease, he fried bread until it was sodden and brown and served it up to me on a big plate and made another trip to the garage.

In the winter, he'd send me out to the garage to start his car so it would be warm when he left for work. He'd make his last cup of instant—spoon in the coffee, pour on the boiling water, and then run in some cold tap water so he could guzzle it down—but before that he'd call to me, call me a name that wasn't my own but that was made up and funny, and flip me his keys.

It was serious business starting the car. The cold night could've run down the battery or the tank could've been a little low, the gas not too clean, and you had to remember to open the garage door so the gouts of exhaust would run to air. Even then the fumes would be thick and floaty and sweet from the cold knocking engine, and you might cough a little, your eyes might water. You couldn't flood the engine, couldn't grind the ignition. You had to do it just right and it was something I got good at.

I remember that, and how sometimes on Saturdays, when he worked a half day and I was eleven or twelve years old, I'd ride to work with him. On the way home he'd let me take over the driving when we came to our road. Later, I was driving him all the way home from his half days on Saturday because that was the safest way for both of us to get home.

He came back in and his glass was full again. I was working my way through the plate of food he'd cooked. My father made a move and almost spilled his drink. I could see him beginning his descent and felt a desperate need to hold him where he was for as long as I could, more so than ever before. Maybe it was because I was leaving in so many ways and had a notion I'd never be coming back again. At the same time, I was angry I'd have to do such a thing.

So I said, "Do you remember when you were in the hospital this winter? Do you remember when I came to see you and you didn't recognize me?" I said that to him.

"No, I'm sorry. I don't remember you coming to see me."

"You thought I was my brother."

"I'm sorry. I don't remember. I don't remember anyone coming to see me."

"What are you going to do?" I asked.

"I don't know," he said. "Eat your breakfast."

He said it in a way that told me it wasn't any of my business what he was going to do next. I appreciated that, him putting me in my place.

"I got something for you," he said, and disappeared down the stairs to the cellar. I kept on laying into those eggs and potatoes, switching the fork to my right hand, which I was not supposed to use, so I could enjoy them more, and then he was behind me.

He said, "Here, take this," tapping me on the shoulder with a blue cane he had from when they took cartilage out of his knee. I told him I was okay, and he kept saying, "You don't want it? You don't want it?"

"Yeah, okay," I said. "I'll take it. It'll be a help." I took the cane and hooked it over the back of the chair. It would be a big help to have it. My foot was sane for the time being, but I knew how later in the day it'd probably call attention to itself.

He nodded and went out to the garage again, starting with an empty glass. When he came back his glass would be full again and his cheeks rosy, his eyes more wet. His head would tilt and then he'd stare and rub his fingers.

He said he could hear someone yelling from the woods but couldn't make out who it was or where it was coming from.

I told him I heard it, too, and he seemed relieved. I told him it was Charley Dickard, but that much he didn't care; he was just relieved that I could hear it, too, so that it wasn't just him hearing something that wasn't there. It was clear to me the talking was over and he was slipping into the deep warm water of his self-medication.

Afton pulled into the driveway, and I stood up quickly and felt my foot flare with heat. She had her grand-mother's blue Falcon. She shut off the engine, and the car rolled ahead, then she remembered to put it in park and I smiled.

"Who's that?" my father said.

He wasn't much for company and got jumpy right away. I told him it was Afton and I went to the door and waved for her to come in. She had never met my father before and they were shy and distant, like people who are afraid of people are when they meet.

Then he got goofy, like a boy, and tried to say polite and charming things, had it in his head he could still be that way. But the liquor was into his brain, and every time he spoke it was the beginning of something polite and charming and then it'd slip away from him. Instead of what he was to say next, he'd say his fifth or sixth thought and not make any sense and then he'd try to turn a joke on himself. It came to be that it was like she was the host, the one trying to make him feel at home in his own house.

So finally he said, "Where are you two off to today?"

"I thought we'd ride up to Fort Ticonderoga."

"I've been up there," he said.

Then came a silence he did not seem to notice and I took a last bite of food and we said our good-byes. I was following her out the door when my father called to me and I went back.

"Hey," he said. "You haven't got a few bucks I could borrow?"

"Sure," I said, and gave him all the money I had in my pockets and left again, hobbling out the door.

Afton was at the passenger side, dangling the keys from her fingers. I told her she should drive because I was supposed to keep my leg and my hand elevated, but mainly I had visions of putting my head in her lap and watching that high blue world through the windshield, maybe falling asleep, maybe putting a hand inside the leg of her shorts.

"You had better drive," she said, tossing me the keys, and that's when she told me she didn't have a driver's license.

"You're twenty years old and you don't have a driver's license?"

I couldn't believe it. A driver's license was like a ticket to freedom for me and I couldn't secure one fast enough when I turned sixteen. I would have stood there and wondered over it with her, asked her why, but my father came out with the cane I had forgotten, came in a hurry and handed it over to me and I thanked him. As we left I could see him in the rearview listening to the woods and then ducking into the side door of the garage.

On the way out of town, we passed by the farm, which looked deserted. I stopped to look for signs of human life but there were none, and then Cy came shuffling from around the barn wearing a sheath knife and holding a pitchfork. I asked what he was doing.

He told me he was watching for that rotten bastard Charley Dickard to show so he could stick him and cut his throat.

I said, "You do that, Cy. You do that."

Then he told me everyone else had disappeared and I believed him, like he really meant they had disappeared, like they had gone to vapor and floated away. He gestured me closer and told me he was convinced it was Charley Dickard what gave the old man the cancer, and when I asked why he thought such a thing he said it was told to him by the old man himself. Said it was the gospel truth.

I stopped at my uncle's filling station for gas and a loan. He was outside with a big handwritten sign that said, SPEED TRAP AHEAD. He was warning the oncoming drivers. It was one of the many services he provided his customers. It was good for business.

He handed me some money and said, "Don't worry about it."

"You know, I stepped on a nail one time, too," he said.

"How do you know I stepped on a nail?"

"You know how word travels."

"Yeah, I guess I do." Then I asked him what he'd heard on Charley Dickard, and he said he'd started up again talking his shit but the old man wouldn't call the constable.

My uncle told me that if it were him, he'd go out and shoot Charley Dickard and he'd be well within his rights.

"Hey," he said. "I heard about your little stunt with the minister."

"Yeah, I know. I shouldn't have done it."

"Ask me, someone ought to shoot his ass, too."

I thanked him for the loan and told him I'd pay him back and he told me again not to worry about it. Afton and I headed up Route 12 to cross the river into Vermont at Bellows Falls, where we climbed from the river valley and turned into the hills. Inside these hills and mountains were the meanders of the streams and rivers and lakes, the shadows like small, deep harbors, the curl of the country roads.

New England is still, for the most part, on a human scale, which is to say the land does not require you to confront it or yourself. It is not so blank as to make you turn to depend on your mind, not so huge that you are dwarfed, not so hospitable that you become wasteful, not so brutal that you die. But of course it's none of this; it's me remembering where I was born and raised and where, for better or worse, I learned to live.

We picked up Route 103 out of Bellows Falls and drove through the raked sunlight, still too low to warm the road and too far from its zenith, when the light would wash into every hollow and valley for some moments before leaving shadow again. We drove through all the little Vermont towns, and it was easy to forget who we were and to make up in our minds who we wanted to be, and it was what I was doing in my mind for the both of us.

In Bellows Falls we'd bought the Sunday *New York Times*, and it was Afton's habit to read the "News of the Week in Review" section, slowly. She wanted it to last. Sometimes, she said, for the holding back of it, for the savoring of it, she didn't finish it until midweek, sometimes not at all. I couldn't understand that, because I wanted everything done yesterday, done before it was started, done and on to the next thing so as to have that done, too.

This was a difference between us I could recognize, my going for the sharp edges of life to knock them off and her letting life come into her of its own accord. Where I was raw and unraveled, she was deliberate and considerable and serene, so often I'd say, What's your opinion, what do you think, how do you see that? And it wasn't just for the stuff of those answers but also to figure out where they came from.

We drove on through the mountains, the road empty because it was Sunday and everyone was in church or at home resting up for Monday. She took out a purse and began to string beads, and miles later she took out threads of silky floss and made string bracelets and fit them around my wrists.

Fort Ticonderoga was smaller than I remembered it from when I was in the second grade, but it was a fine sunny day and a breeze was coming off the lake and the surrounding land seemed to be cut into the sky. We paid our money and wandered in among the crowd of people who'd come to be here for their own reasons. We passed in front of the high south wall, its bronze cannon facing Lake Champlain.

We held hands and walked slowly because of my foot and because, too, in this place of gray stone it was as if time was sending us backwards. We had all the time in the world that had ever been. Children were climbing on the cannons and dashing along the parapets, yelling to one another from across the bastions. There were more cannons inside, iron and brass and mortars. In the barracks were museums of surgery, guns, clothing, people.

Late afternoon we watched them load a cannon for a demonstration. The target was a fifty-five-gallon barrel. A young guy about our age barked out orders, then turned to the crowd of us and explained what all he had just said. When they were about ready to fire the cannon, the guy told how it was a tradition to invite a person, a woman, to sight and shoot the cannon, and then he came into the crowd and asked Afton if she'd be the one. She was embarrassed, but what can you do in a situation like that? Everybody was looking at us like they wished they were us but were happy, at the same time, that they weren't, because people don't go in much for that sort of attention.

"Don't worry," he said. "We'll help you," and then, all gentlemanlike, he took her hand by the fingers and escorted her to the firing line.

She bent at the waist and I could see her moving her fingers a little this way, a little that way, and when they touched the cannon off, it made a great whoomph and the shell heaved from its muzzle and did not hit the barrel.

Then he told how they had never hit the barrel and everybody laughed and applauded. When she came back to me, she took my arm and I was proud of her for being picked to shoot the cannon.

From the fort, we drove farther into New York State, and it was as if everywhere we went we were the first, the discoverers. We stopped at a place on Schroon Lake called The Narrows and ate pizza. A fan ticked over our heads and it was all intoxicating to me, the smell of pizza-making, and the lake out the window, and whiffs of suntan oil, and all the pretty women and handsome men dressed so daring because it was August and New York State.

We must have seemed like we were a long-married couple, what with me and my cane and the quietness and calmness that attended her whenever she walked, wherever she walked. We sat beside each other and did not talk. We ate pizza and looked about the room as if it were all new and mysterious, as if we were visiting from Paris, France, or Jupiter. We were not out of reach or touch, and she tended my wrist with her looks and her fingers on my forearm and insisted I keep my leg across her lap.

And then I'd remember how we were in a seam of life on this very day and would soon be pulled from it by our ambitions, by the roads we were on, the plans we'd made, and what we thought was important in life. When she would touch me again, I'd be aware of her touch and come back to her. We decided to stay the night, to not go back. It was my idea. At first she said we couldn't do that, and I said we'd have to call and say we were having car trouble. She said okay. So we got a motel room, the second I'd ever stayed in.

I liked the room. It had what we needed but no history, no evidence of who came before, and the only claim it made on our lives was a few dollars. I called home and got my father, and he seemed to just take it as news, without asking for details. Afton called her grandmother and felt bad telling the lie because the woman was concerned for her safety, felt so very bad when she heard that it was her car causing the trouble.

We walked the streets that night, me on my bum foot, and stopped at a bar. A guy there had a guitar and everybody was singing. We ate peanuts and drank beer and, on the way back to the room, stopped at a drugstore for magazines and newspapers, and a roll of gauze to change the bandage on my wrist, and Epsom salts because I was supposed to soak my foot, and incense and candles to burn in the room. We bought beer and filled the sink with ice to keep it cold. I sat up on the bed and read and jotted down my thoughts, feeling them to be important because they were coming to me during an important time.

Afton lay beside me reading. She'd be on some page of the *New York Times* and read, "The blackpole warbler flies nonstop from Maine to Venezuela in eighty to one hundred hours and weighs less than half an ounce," and then she fell asleep with her head on my lap. I soon ran out of important thoughts, so I got myself up and pulled on my blue jeans. I wanted to wake her, to not be alone, but I didn't, and I surely did not want to go to sleep myself, because I didn't want this day to ever end.

I took a beer and went outside and sat in a wooden chair by the door. The beer made me feel tired, and my wrist began to ache for the first time that day. I unwrapped it to let the air get to it, to take a look at the damage I'd done myself. In all, there were sixteen stitches, and tied loosely across them was the turquoise and blue and pink string bracelet she'd braided on the drive up.

I went back in to check on her and it was like coming home. I woke her up and tried to tell her this and it came out not making much sense, so I asked her to change the bandage for me. She said she would in a minute and got up and went into the bathroom. Without closing the door she sat down to pee and we looked at each other and laughed because we were in the time when just about everything we did was for the first or second time. I went to where she was and kissed her and took another beer from the sink and sat down outside in the cool, piney air to wait for her.

When she came out she was wearing my T-shirt, which went down to her thighs, and she sat in my lap and curled her body to mine wherever she could. She took my beer and had a sip, and I told her my father used to make his own beer and how I wasn't very good at numbers then, still am not, but I remember that when I was in the second grade and a can of malt was sixty-six cents he'd be in the kitchen making his home brew and say, What's the number? I didn't know and then he'd turn it around to make it ninety-nine cents and he'd say, What's that number? and I'd say we hadn't learned those numbers in school yet. I meant for it to be a funny story, but to her it was sad.

I sighed and let my head go back and must have dozed off sitting there on that hard wooden chair, and there are so many nights in my life when I wish sleep would come in just that way, sudden and quiet and complete.

"Come on, lazybones," she was saying. "Come inside. Come to bed." And she was tugging me and getting me to my feet. I came awake and felt rested, and we went inside and lit the candles and the incense so that jasmine took over the pine. She unbuttoned my blue jeans and slid them down and I stepped out of them. Then I lifted my T-shirt over her head and felt her fingers on my chest and neck and down my back and my thighs. She pulled me against her and we lay down on the bed.

"This incense," she said. "I was in the town of Selinunte, on the point of Sicily that faces Africa. It used to be an ancient Greek port city. One afternoon when the sun was setting, it was a perfect night. There was this temple from the fifth century B.C., mostly only columns, and I was all alone. It was lit up at night. The light came out of the ground from below. Am I making sense?"

"Yes," I said, holding her more, not caring if she made sense or not, trusting she did.

"So I was walking alone toward the temple and there was a full canopy of stars. I could hear the ocean and the waves. It was so quiet, perfectly still. I stopped about fifty yards from the temple and heard this hooting, these long hoots. There weren't any trees around, none at all, and then this huge owl flew right out from inside the temple. It flew out from the very center, toward the ocean, and disappeared into the night, and you know what?"

"What?"

"It was Athena's owl. It was there for me. Life does that,

fixes itself for me in moments so I can know it. It makes sense of itself for me."

"Maybe it had a nest in there."

"I went back the next day and there was no sign of a nest and no place really where it could have had a nest."

"But they have their nests in places where it doesn't seem like they'd be on purpose."

"But what difference does it make? It would only be all the better if the owl lived there anyway."

"What's it mean?"

"The owl was the symbol of wisdom and prophecy."

"What did it tell you?" I asked.

She didn't say anything and I remembered my father taking me outdoors at dusk to hear the whippoorwill off in the forest and saying its name. It's a night bird, too.

I never saw a whippoorwill, but I heard it say its name. I remember my father talking to the whippoorwill, calling its name back to it and asking me, Did you hear it? Did you hear it? as if his life depended on it. Barefoot and wearing just my skivvies, I'd fidget and rock in the dew-white grass, the lawn sparkling like clear dark marbles in the sun.

My mother would call out from the house, want to know what we were doing. She'd say, Bring him in here. She'd say, He's going to catch his death of cold.

My father would be wearing a white T-shirt and green trousers and black shoes, and he'd be holding a beer bottle against his thigh, pointed towards the night-blue sky. He'd tell her, Just a minute, say it impatiently, kind of growl the words, and we'd stare at the black profile of the woods at the foot of the lawn. The air was cold at night, even in summer, and it smelled of pine and cut hay. I'd move closer to my father and breathe him in. He smelled like sweat and the sun, smelled faintly of grease and machine oil and tobacco, and I hoped I was just like him and always would be.

"Sometimes these things can't be explained," she said. "I'm leaving tomorrow or the next day. I have to be back at Oswego this week."

In that moment I saw Afton flying through the air to Oswego, and then I was there, too, and I was sad because we weren't flying at all.

"Okay," she said. "First you were smiling and then you were sad. It went right across your face. I could see it."

"It'll be fine," I said. "We'll write. I'll come visit."

"Love letters," she said.

I went to kiss her and she held me back.

"Listen to me. Listen to what I'm telling you. You have to trust this," she said. "We have our lives to get on with."

"Yes, we have to be getting on with our lives," I said. "Yes, we'll write, we'll be in touch whenever we can."

By and by we fell asleep, and when we woke up, high in the Adirondack Mountains, her shoulder blades went to wings as she rose and fell. She made small sounds and took my fingers in her mouth to keep from crying out and settled down into me, curled and folded and closed and opened to me. That was the night we made love in the air.

I Fall to Pieces

THERE ARE SO many stories I have left undone, left incomplete—the story of how we lifted the stone, the fate of Charley Dickard, the aerial photograph, the death of Billy—but to leave a little bit undone, a little bit unfinished, is to leave something for the morning, a reason to come awake.

I'll tell this much more. When we returned from New York State, nothing was said to me about being away the night, and it was like something had been broken free. The old man wanted to know when I'd be able to come back to work, so I guessed that for the time being I wasn't fired anymore. Charley Dickard disappeared and has been gone ever since. It was like any other night had passed and there was no reason to remember its passing.

On Tuesday, I drove Afton and her grandmother down to Rhode Island. Her grandmother took a liking to me and so felt free to be highly critical of my driving. She gave me the rundown on the family, including her brother who joined the navy too young and went on to hunt water moccasins for the state of Connecticut. He'd catch them by the tail and whip them in the air to snap their necks. He, too, had cauterized his own leg in the woods with a red-hot ax. All the while she was talking, she was doing the *New York Times* crossword puzzle in ink. She didn't seem daffy until the next morning, when I had to be introduced to her all over again. She would go on to outlive a lot of people I knew.

In Rhode Island I was like a prize Afton had brought home. We spent the day on the beach and my white legs took a burning in the sun, and that evening we walked the narrow streets of Newport and drank cold beer and ate so many fried clams we had bellyaches. Late that night we ended up back on the beach, wading in the black snarl of water making its low growl at sand's edge.

In September, Afton would call me from Oswego to tell me she was pregnant, and I'd disappear from school for a week with fifteen brand-new twenties in my pocket and hitchhike out there to be with her. It was money my uncle would give me, and he wouldn't ask what I needed it for. She had an apartment off campus, and I stayed the week and would have stayed for as long as she wanted me to. It was something we didn't talk about afterwards; it was just something between the two of us.

Years later, after my father died, after Billy died, I was in Heber, Utah, in August when I saw my first ghost. I was riding alone in America, traveling by land, traveling

by motorcycle, considering the run to Sturgis, South Da-
kota. My father had traveled through Heber when he was
nineteen, and he'd been dead for a few years, and that was
part of why I was out there.

It was cold. When the sun goes down it gets cold, and
before it comes up it gets even colder. I should have been
home where I lived, but you reach those points in life
where you spend more time looking backwards, because
you've learned to have faith in the slender record of time
and place and event, faith that it will deliver itself up to
you and faith that it sometimes can be possessed.

My grandfather's will was such a thing. It was a doc-
ument that in the end tied us to the land, for it said that
to sell any piece of the land would alter the inheritance.
It didn't matter, because, whether we liked it or not, we'd
already tied ourselves to the land and that knot was pulled
tight hundreds of years ago.

So there in Heber, in a motel room under the cuff
of a moon, I was reading my maps, reading whatever
newspapers I could get my hands on. I had just eaten the
special at Chick's Place across the street: chicken-fried
steak, mashed potatoes, succotash, and a scone as big as
your fist.

The waitress was young and pretty, like a daughter. She
said, Go with the special, you can't go wrong. She said it
as if she knew me, knew my life, knew the things I was
afraid of. She wanted to know where I'd been and where
I was going. She liked to bring me food. She called me
hon, like a good waitress does, but was too young to get
away with it.

After supper, I was sitting at the table in the room reading about the stars, reading how back in 1979 Liza Minnelli was afraid of being victimized by Skylab. Back then, newspapers were full of reports that chunks of orbiting space laboratory would be plummeting to earth and that no one knew where they were going to land, and Liza Minnelli, who, according to this article was using drugs and drinking at the time, was afraid she would be hit. Her friend Halston talked her out of it. They spent the weekend at his house on Long Island. He took her out onto the porch and said, That's where it will hit.

Look, he said, pointing to the ocean, that's where Skylab is going to hit and won't it be fabulous? And you and I are going to pull up a couple of chairs and watch it.

They had a lovely meal and the fear of Skylab never bothered her again.

I began remembering my own life with Skylab. While Liza Minnelli and Halston were sitting on a porch on Long Island, me and Billy were sitting in a thousand acres of watermelons somewhere east of Floresville, Texas. We were building high line, working for Seaward Construction out of Kittery, Maine. We were surrounded by watermelons, parked between two drops of tower steel, parked where the span would sag. We were parked there because a storm had come up and ball lightning was raising hell all around us. There'd be great snaps and showers of sparks, cascades of flame as the lightning hit the half-erected steel skeletons.

We were young and still single. We were working five twelve-hour days and an eight on Saturday. Still enough time on the weekend to wash your face and head north to San Antonio, or maybe south to Corpus Christi, or down to Matamoros.

We lived in a trailer where a woman had lived and then disappeared, leaving behind most all her belongings. Her clothes were in a drawer, her dresses in the closet, and there were a few spices in the rack. I opened the medicine cabinet like you do when you're in someone else's bathroom, and it was a woman's medicine cabinet. There were files and brushes, powder, shadows, paints, blush and polish, witch hazel, tiger balm, wintergreen, coltsfoot candy, anise seeds, muslin bags of lovage leaves. There were strands of hair and a space on the second shelf where something used to be, something she took with her, I wondered what it was.

The time we spent there, we did not disturb her things, did not so much unpack ourselves as live from our knapsacks, but in a way I did disturb her things by writing down everything she had in her medicine cabinet, the words good as photographs.

Down in Texas I loved driving at night and there'd always be some one of us drunk and rolling around in the back of the pickup. Or sitting in lawn chairs drinking Pearl Beer or Lone Star, tasting that cool, sweet air. Driving south was a long downhill, an illusion of sorts, with lights splashed in the distance and, between you and the light, inky darkness, my mind made out to be black water. I'd ask everyone I met if driving south was like a long downhill and they'd say yes, they'd experienced it, too. It was an illusion of sorts. I wrote in my journal how people in Texas experience their illusions. I wrote, *What a great country this must be. America the beautiful.*

On the fourth of July we went down to Port Aransas and camped out on the beach. I got so burned I was laid up for two days, blisters like water bags on my shins.

On one of those laid-up nights, Billy took me to a swimming pool to find some relief from the pain. We climbed the fence and slid on in. I thought I was going to drown. My legs felt like they weighed a thousand pounds, like carp or catfish on a long line, like I was dragging a dead man. I made for the ladder and got onto the concrete. The blisters had filled with pool water and were now leaking it back out in thin streams, like one of those little Roman statues pissing in a fountain. Billy came up the ladder behind me. Seems he opened his eyes underwater and his contacts floated out and away. He was new to contacts, and I guess he didn't know you weren't supposed to open your eyes underwater.

Saturday nights we'd head up to San Antonio and dance with all the girls, girls named Serefina and Nina. They wore squash-blossom necklaces, their long black hair knotted in *chongos*, their eyes like coffee beans. I remember Serefina wanted to become a witch in the worst way but didn't know the first thing about it. Serefina and Nina and me and Billy and Ernest Tubb, *I could waltz across Texas with you* . . . and Patsy Cline, *I fall to pieces.*

There was more lightning that day and our crew was huddled in the back of the ten-wheeler. Me and Billy were wondering about where Skylab might come down, had read where this was one of the possible locations.

Billy was saddened by the declining orbit of Skylab. He was pissed off that NASA had turned into such a bunch of fuckups, and was convinced it'd not be so if his own life had gone differently.

In the back our crew had a scorpion and a tarantula in a gallon jug. Every time the scorpion plunged its abdomen over its head, they'd yell out, Eeeee-yah, eeeee-yah, delighted by the show. Most of them were illegals, friendly without choice, good company for Skylab watching. I told them it was Skylab falling all around us and thought they believed me. They told me I had a black-widow spider on my shoulder. They were right, I was wrong.

Later that season we left Texas and almost died in the mountains in Kentucky. Billy was driving the El Camino and I was asleep. We were barreling through the fog and darkness under the sky's low ceiling, going fast because we were headed home. He wanted to stop in and see Carol and I wanted to see Afton. In my dreams were the lights of soda machines we'd seen in Birmingham, bright torches of gas wells in the fields of Shreveport. We were headed home, cross-country on the diagonal.

What woke me up I'll never know. Let's just say it was one of those times you wake up when you should wake up. Like needing to wake up at five a.m. and doing it without an alarm.

What I woke to was our heading into the red eyes of a parked trailer truck. I hit the steering wheel and my hand kept going and I punched Billy in the chest and woke him up, too. The El Camino careened down the road, poising on two wheels for swift, lunging moments before whipsawing to its opposite wheels. I could see stars below me, the lights of a town, the same town again and again. We pulled over and stopped and kissed the ground. We did that and got back in and headed out again.

Back home they were in the last days of the death watch. The old man would have that fall and winter and would die on Easter Sunday in 1980. After he died, people started bringing in cows from four different states and two provinces. Cows came from around the countryside from people we didn't even know. It had been his habit to board cows with young farmers and farmers a little down on their luck, and in return for boarding them, they milked the cows they otherwise could not afford. When he sold those cows, he'd move some new ones onto their farm for them to milk. When he died, so many cows came home we didn't know where to put them all.

When I saw him late that summer in 1979, I wanted to ask him about the aerial photograph. Somehow it must have been lost or destroyed, because it was never found, although people have filled in its absence. People have made up its presence. Everyone in the family re-members it, remembers having seen it, and even knows when and where they saw it. They can tell you it hung in the hallway or the stairway or the sitting room and it was there for this many years, and they'll say, Don't you remember it?

But they couldn't have seen it, because when the aerial photo finally came the old man studied it and then he hid it away. That late summer day, I wanted to ask him where it was and how it had come out in the end and was Charley Dickard in it, but I couldn't bring myself to do that what with him dying and all.

Some years later, Billy died in an accident like the one we almost had in Kentucky. He'd married Carol by then and he called her baby doll. They had a son who was bow-legged and who toddle-walked like his father. It was in the Wasatch where he died, not far from Heber, not far from where I was on that night a few years before.

When I got the news of his death, I was living in Conquest, New York. I'd just gotten in from the heifer barn and my mother was on the phone. She'd heard the news and was passing it on. It was like my stomach started floating, the way a magician levitates a beautiful woman, and then it slammed into my neck. That's where it hurt the most, in my neck and shoulders, like after a day on a roof or in a ditch or baling hay.

I don't know for sure the details, but this is how I think he died. It was a weekday. It was late at night and he was coming off the line after maybe five twelves. You get tired after pulling a shift like that. You learn to sleep anywhere, to sleep whenever you can.

So he was coming off a mountain that night, and out there the mountains are abrupt and unforgiving. They don't give a fuck about you or me, and he was thinking about Carol and his son. He had loved Carol ever since he met her in the eighth grade, but it was a long time before she took notice enough to marry him. He'd write her letters when we were down in Texas. He'd read them to me, get my opinion, because I'd been an English major. She was married at the time to someone else and not happy.

Those letters must have become her salvation. They must have started fires.

That night, coming out of the Wasatch, he was thinking, too, about the project he had in mind, where he'd build the first power line to the moon that was following him off that mountain. He had spoken to me about it before. To him, this was serious thought, filled with intent and desire. He wasn't a kid thinking anymore, and neither was I.

That was when the logging truck ran over his pickup, when he was tired and dreamy, thinking about Carol and his son and being a lineman to the moon.

In my daring moments I wonder if he hurt. He was of a small build and tough and didn't feel pain in any normal way. He'd walk around with a broken bone or a gash in his arm and wouldn't even know about it.

I don't care about the death of famous people much, but he was famous to me. I think how someone wasn't there to grab the wheel for him that night in Utah. If I'd been there, he wouldn't be dead, and if it hadn't been for Liza Minnelli, I wouldn't have been remembering all this. So I think about Liza Minnelli, too, how she's peeling a shrimp or languid in sleep, her arms shifting to positions of rest, show tunes printed on her brain.

I was looking for the feeling of cure out in the air when the ghost came. It was my father. He was wearing his shop clothes: black shoes, his pants a saturation of green, a blazing white T-shirt, his smokes rolled in the sleeve. It was how I sometimes saw him in my mind, and he'd be doing something, like holding a torch up to a nest of caterpillars at night, burning them out of the tree so they couldn't destroy it.

It's how I remember him best, before he got promoted and took to wearing a bow tie and plaid sports jacket. He worked for a company that made screws, nuts, bolts, and washers. When I was a kid and would go into the factory with him on Saturdays there'd be only me and him and a few guys pushing out an order, a few guys making overtime.

He'd take me around to every machine and drop a handful of what it was making into a sack for me. These go to Harrison Radiator, he'd say, and these go to West-inghouse. The sack would get heavier. These are half-inch, 8-32 roundhead brass, chromium-plated machine screws.

There were roundhead, flathead, oval head, fillister head, square head, hexagon head, and a dozen more. There were square nuts, jam nuts, castellated nuts, wing nuts, and washers, flat, split, and shake-proof, and everything came in a variety of lengths, diameters, and pitch.

When I was in the second grade was when we drove to Fort Ticonderoga. It was the only vacation we ever took. It wasn't until last year that I found out it was because he came home in pretty bad shape and my mother didn't trust him anymore. Going to the factory on Saturdays be-came our vacations.

But the ghost, it was my father telling me he'd seen Billy and all was well.

"Yourself?" I said.

"Can't complain," he said.

My father said to me then, "Our souls have suffered in a kind of darkness."

I thought. Yes, I have figured that out.

His presence lingered, and that night I stayed awake to be weary, because I've found that only weariness can purify, only weariness can give rest to the wicked, only the dead can sustain the living.

Down there in the state of Texas, me and Billy would watch all of television for the night—the news and the late movies. The news was always about death in Houston, oil spills in the gulf, a petrochemical plant headed skyward, illegals found dead in a boxcar on a siding. Then I'd go up to the mailbox, treading through the crickets and grasshoppers that swarmed the ground, and open the steel slot and let slide in a letter to Afton.

Parked in the shadows there'd be a Texas ranger, and I'd stop and talk with him, draw him out a little and be impressed with all his shootouts. I would want to ask him if he knew about the woman who used to live where we lived, but then I wouldn't want to know what he might know about her. We'd talk a bit about the weather and how you got to be a Texas ranger and where he was from and where I was from.

One night, when I got back to the trailer, Billy was reading my journal and he told me how much he liked it. He said he'd been reading it right along and expected any day for me to just open my mouth and start speaking like the words on the page.

Me and Billy laughed because at the time we didn't know how the story would be about him and me, about all of us.

That summer I traveled back to Afton, and later, from Utah, I traveled back to her again, and every night I fold myself into her, every night she comes into my life and I feel her hand on my heart and she is saying, I am here . . . I am here. This is all what I know now, and how can that not make different what I knew then?

Robert Olmstead is the author of eight previous books, including novels, a short story collection, and this memoir. *Coal Black Horse* was the winner of the Heartland Prize for Fiction. *The Coldest Night* was a finalist for the Dayton Literary Peace Prize. *Far Bright Star* was the winner of the Western Writers of America Spur Award. Olmstead is the recipient of a Guggenheim Fellowship and an NEA grant. A native of New Hampshire, he is a professor at Ohio Wesleyan University.

Brock Clarke is the author of seven works of fiction, including the bestselling *An Arsonist's Guide to Writers' Homes in New England*, as well as the essay collection *I, Grape; or The Case for Fiction*. He lives in Maine and teaches at Bowdoin College.

A NOTE ON THE TYPE

Stay Here with Me has been set in Caslon. This modern version is based on the early-eighteenth-century roman designs of the British printer William Caslon I, whose typefaces were so popular that they were employed for the first setting of the Declaration of Independence, in 1776. Eric Gill's humanist typeface Gill Sans, from 1928, has been used for display.

Book Design & Composition by Tammy Ackerman

GODINE NONPAREIL
Celebrating the joy of discovery with books bound to be classics.

Godine's Nonpareil paperback series features essential works by great authors—from stand-alone books of nonfiction and fiction to collections of essays, stories, interviews, and letters—introduced by celebrated contemporary voices who have deep connections to the featured authors and their trove of work.

ANN BEATTIE More to Say: Essays & Appreciations
Selected and Introduced by the author

HENRY BESTON Herbs and the Earth
Introduction by Roger B. Swain and Afterword by Bill McKibben

GUY DAVENPORT The Geography of the Imagination: Forty Essays
Introduction by John Jeremiah Sullivan

ANDRE DUBUS The Lieutenant: A Novel
Afterword by Andre Dubus III

MAVIS GALLANT Paris Notebooks: Essays & Reviews
Foreword by Hermione Lee

WILLIAM MAXWELL The Writer as Illusionist: Uncollected & Unpublished Work
Selected and Introduced by Alec Wilkinson

JAMES ALAN MCPHERSON On Becoming an American Writer: Nonfiction & Essays
Selected and Introduced by Anthony Walton

BHARATI MUKHERJEE Darkness: Stories
Introduction by the author and Afterword by Clark Blaise

ROBERT OLMSTEAD Stay Here with Me: A Memoir
Introduction by Brock Clarke

ADELE CROCKETT ROBERTSON The Orchard: A Memoir
Foreword by Betsy Robertson Cramer and Afterword by Jane Brox

ALISON ROSE Better Than Sane: Tales from a Dangling Girl
Introduction by Porochista Khakpour

ALEC WILKINSON Midnights: A Year with the Wellfleet Police
Foreword by William Maxwell and Afterword by the author

ALEC WILKINSON Moonshine: A Life in Pursuit of White Liquor
Introduction by Padgett Powell and Afterword by the author

MONICA WOOD Any Bitter Thing: A Novel
Introduction by Cathie Pelletier